Illustrated Guide to
Snowmobile Racing

Linda and David Aksomitis

Iconografix

Iconografix
PO Box 446
Hudson, Wisconsin 54016 USA

Library of Congress Control Number: 2006922856

ISBN-13: 978-1-58388-170-5
ISBN-10: 1-58388-170-0

06 07 08 09 10 11 6 5 4 3 2 1

Printed in China

Cover and book design by Dan Perry

On the cover:
Top left- Jacques Villeneuve, three-time World Champion oval racer from Quebec.
Top right- Watercross racer at Grantsburg, Wisconsin.
Lower left- Snocross race at West Yellowstone, Montana.
Lower right- Ice drag racer at Fort Qu'Appelle, Saskatchewan.
Center- Aaron Christensen, Pro Snocross driver from Alberta.

Book Proposals

Iconografix is a publishing company specializing in books for transportation enthusiasts. We publish in a number of different areas, including Automobiles, Auto Racing, Buses, Construction Equipment, Emergency Equipment, Farming Equipment, Railroads & Trucks. The Iconografix imprint is constantly growing and expanding into new subject areas.

Authors, editors, and knowledgeable enthusiasts in the field of transportation history are invited to contact the Editorial Department at Iconografix, Inc., PO Box 446, Hudson, WI 54016.

CONTENTS

DEDICATION

This book is dedicated to the many thousands of snowmobile racers, teams, and promoters whose stories and accomplishments are untold—they are the foundation of the sport.

ABOUT THE AUTHORS

Linda and David Aksomitis spent a decade through the 1980s and early 1990s participating in snowmobile racing events from Alberta to Ontario, and North Dakota to Michigan. Now the owners of *SnowRider Online Magazine*, they travel across the snowzone covering race events and hitting the snowmobile and ATV trails.

ACKNOWLEDGMENTS

We'd like to express our thanks to the many people and organizations who helped us bring this book together:
- Rosemary Daver, our research assistant
- Gerard Aksomitis for the many ways he contributed to the final product
- Loren Anderson, for his expertise and assistance
- The International Snowmobile Hall of Fame and Museum, St. Germain, Wisconsin
- The Blair Morgan Racing Team, especially Wayne Madsen
- Jason Gilmour of snoxmagazine.com
- John McNally and the volunteers involved with the Grantsburg Watercross event
- Gene Shaw and the volunteers involved with the Duluth National Snocross event
- Ernie Nairn and the Canadian Open Snocross event organizers in Winnipeg
- Dale Neduzak and the many volunteers at the Canadian Power Toboggan Championships
- The Decker family and all of the volunteers at the Eagle River Derby Track
- Marysue and the West Yellowstone Chamber of Commerce; Marge with the West Yellowstone Expo; and the RMXCRC Snocross organizers and volunteers
- Kelly Barbello and the Jackson Hole Chamber of Commerce; the Jackson Hole Snow Devils volunteers at the annual Jackson Hole World Championship Hill Climb; the racers and organizers from the RMSHA
- Garry Kainz and the Snow Leopards Family Snowmobile Club and their Vintage Racing events
- Sintaluta Grass Drags volunteers & organizers
- Fort Qu'Appelle Snowmobile Drag Racing event organizers and the SSRA
- NSDRA asphalt drag racing association members
- WPSA event organizers

FOREWORD

By Loren R. Anderson, Founder and President, Snowmobile Hall of Fame and Museum, St. Germain, Wisconsin

Linda and David Aksomitis have written what many will call the continuation of the Bill Vint story "Warriors of Winter" first published in 1977. In many ways it is just that. Linda and David bring us right up to the present day racing scene played out every weekend in the snow belt of the United States and Canada during what I call the "white-gold" season. For the economies of many snow-belt communities, snowmobiling and snowmobile racing are vital. With this said however, there just is not a lot of money involved in the sport. For most racers, it takes a total commitment to their checkered flag pursuits. The high paid "factory drivers" are few and far between. Snowmobile racers must be dedicated and must be willing to give up a lot for their dreams.

This book details the types of racing venues and gives many examples of the exciting ski- to ski racing that has made the sport so riveting to so many sledheads. When one witnesses an organized, professional race event, we often take the action and all the preparation for granted. Snowmobilers are a unique and dedicated group. At the local and state club levels, it is volunteers that build and maintain the trails and bridges, fight the easement problems and the govern-

ment issues too. In the racing arena, many have no idea of the dedication and commitment made by drivers, crews, sponsors and race organizers. Snowmobile racing is a family sport and is held together by the same threads that hold families together.

Most racers have full time jobs that are not related to the sport. They work evenings and burn the midnight oil to be ready to load the trailer and head off each Friday for another weekend of racing. Most have all volunteer crews. For most, mom, dad and other family members make up these dedicated warriors. Toss in a few friends and neighbors and you have a snowmobile race team. Sure there are a few big name big buck teams, but the likes of Blair Morgan Racing or Moyle Racing are the exceptions to the rule.

The sacrifices made by snowmobile racing families and friends are the real backbone of the sport. The Snowmobile Hall of Fame and Museum in St. Germain, Wisconsin exists to honor and showcase these many heroes. This book helps deliver the praise and respect earned by the racing community. It is these great unpaid and dedicated warriors that make racing what it is today. Thank you Linda and David for giving us this exciting insight and current snapshot of our great sport.

INTRODUCTION

Snowmobiles are the most versatile machine man ever invented—or perhaps the racers who drive them are the most innovative. Whichever the case, the combination of competitive spirit, and a machine with the potential for virtually unlimited speed and flexibility, has created a sport that spans every terrain and season: snowmobile racing.

Exactly who invented the snowmobile is a much-debated question. Was it, as Canadians claim, Joseph Armand Bombardier, in Valcourt, Quebec in 1922? Or was it invented when the U.S. patent for the snowmobile was registered by Virgil D. White, for his Ford car conversion skis and caterpillar-type track, which was granted in 1913? Perhaps the true invention of the snowmobile was the patent granted to Wisconsin inventor Carl Eliason in 1927, for the first single-track, one passenger machine—his motor toboggan. Then there was the much earlier 1896 patent awarded to Moses, William, and Joseph Runnue of Crested Butte, Colorado for their power sled that had an endless track.

Popular opinion seems to consider Bombardier, like Ford with the automobile, as the inventor, since he was the first to mass produce single rider snowmobiles. Ski-Doo, originally to be called the Ski-Dog, rolled 225 units off the assembly line for the fall of 1959. However, even here there's a glitch in history. David Johnson, one of three partners who owned Polaris Industries, built a single seater snow machine in the winter of 1955. Edgar Hetteen, another of the partners, saw the potential and soon Polaris was building sleds—first called Sno-Cats and Pol-Cats, and finally Sno-Travelers. They built 75 units in 1956-1957, and increased the number to more than 300 in 1957-1958. Polaris Industries, still situated in Roseau, Minnesota, produced more sleds per season than Bombardier, two years before the Ski-Doo line was sold.

Hetteen soon left Polaris to start up his own company, Polar Manufacturing, at nearby Thief River Falls. This became the Arctic Cat line. His first Polar 500, an all-season, all-terrain vehicle was produced in December 1961 and cost buyers the grand sum of $1,210.00.

These pioneers of snowmobile history—who all contributed to making the snowmobile what it is today—have been recognized by the Snowmobile Hall of Fame. Bombardier was inducted in the second year, 1989; Hetteen in 1990; and Eliason in 1991. More recent inventors who provided a new revolutionary design, the Karpiks of Eveleth, Minnesota, patented the Blade in 1999. Gerard, Brian and David created the first new snowmobile manufacturer in decades. They had already invented the M-10 suspension, so a snowmobile was the logical next step.

But what of racing? Some say the first snowmobile race was held the day they made the second snowmobile, while the first organized snowmobile race seems to have been held on January 31, 1926 on Rangeline Lake, which is near Three Lakes, Wisconsin. Of course, these 1926 snowmobiles were car conversions rather than single seater motor toboggans.

Three decades later, Hetteen and Johnson, trying to create a market for their snowmobiles, took the machines to where they'd be of the greatest advantage to people: Northern Canada. They unloaded a pair of Sno-Travelers at the 1957 Trapper's Festival held annually in The Pas, Manitoba. Here, the machines competed not against each other, but against sled dog teams. The Sno-Traveler victory produced a Winnipeg order for 25 machines, ensuring the continuation of the fledgling business. But more important, it set a hands-on standard that was to dominate snowmobile promotion and development by manufacturers. Each innovation was born, then tested, on the snowmobile racetrack.

Over the decades many have been dedicated to the sport of snowmobile racing, with none more involved than Mike Trapp, C. J. Ramstad, and Loren Anderson, who came up with the idea for a Hall of Fame and Museum in 1983. Mike was a two-time Eagle River World champion and Loren had been a number one bib in open and 650 classes. CJ, already one of the sport's historians, had a photo library telling the thrilling history of racing. Today their dream—the Snowmobile Hall of Fame and Museum—honors the men and women who've contributed to the sport, as well as displaying their unique and exciting sleds.

The Snowmobile Hall of Fame has a 20-acre Hall of Fame campus situated just west of Eagle River, Wisconsin in St. Germain. The Hall of Fame Museum is open year round. Championship sleds on display include oval, enduro, hill-climb, cross-country, water-cross, snow-cross and drag sleds raced by championship drivers such as Karpik, Wicht, Musselman, Coltom, Hayes, Elsner, Solem, Bernat, Frandsen, Nelson, Bender, Maki, Hibbert, Morgan and Vincent. The first prototype Chaparral built by Keith Huber and an early 1946 Eliason are also on display. Individuals and businesses may become lifetime members of the Hall of Fame to support the history of this wonderful sport.

This photo is just one small section of the amazing contents of the Hall of Fame Museum, situated just outside St. Germain, Wisconsin. The museum is dedicated to preserving and showcasing the rich and exciting history of snowmobiling at both the recreational and competitive levels through the operation of a museum, hall of fame and library for the sport. Annual inductions honor the men and women that have played significant roles at the racing venues, design and manufacturing arenas, local clubs, state associations and national organizations.

Chapter 1
EXTREME RACING ON SNOW

Extreme racing on snow has built snowmobile racing to what it is today as a spectator sport, with its inclusion in events like the X Games and coverage of the WPSA Snocross events on International television. Whether it's snocross or hillcross, the events are crowd pleasers, with snowmobiles flying through the air and racing ski-to-ski with lots of bumping and jostling for position.

The Events

Snocross has gradually become the most popular form of snowmobile racing. Over the years many various spellings have been used for this sport, in-cluding SnoCross, snowcross, snow cross, Sno-Cross, and snow-cross. The most common is snocross, since it is used by the WPSA or World PowerSports Association whose hard work has brought snowmobile racing to the forefront of winter sporting events. The WPSA (called the WSA or World Snowmobile Association until the fall of 2005) is a governing body that organizes, promotes, and regulates a variety of snowmobile competitions. These competitions include the popular Snocross series, along with the emerging Hillcross® series. Sno-Cross events are also sanctioned by the USSA (United States Snowmobile Association), which is the world's oldest sanctioning

Close competition is what brings everyone to the snocross track, and these two drivers are about as close as you can get as they jump the hill on Duluth's Spirit Mountain racetrack.

The first corner in snocross is the most important, since the field of as many as ten drivers all jump to action when the flag drops and head simultaneously into the corner. There's lots of tipping and banging into one another as the drivers keep their throttles pinned, trying to emerge as first out of the corner. Here you can see how driver Aaron Christensen uses his left leg to push up the sled and avert a rollover.

body, along with a few other smaller organizations.

One of the most important snocross events of the year is the annual competition at the X Games. When the games were created by ESPN (Entertainment and Sports Programming Network) in 1995 they covered just summer events, with a mandate to provide an international competition site for participants in extreme sports. The name changed from Extreme Games to X Games in January, 1996, with a winter competition added in 1997. Broadcast to 198 countries and territories in 21 different languages, their popularity continued to grow, so the expanded slate of winter classes in 1998 included SnoCross.

A snocross event takes advantage of a natural terrain or uses a man-made track, and often, even man-made snow for the season openers. The snocross track consists of tight turns, sharp bermed corners, and a variety of bumps and moguls, which allow drivers to catch big air. Snocross racers often reach heights of 30 feet (9 metres) after launching off a huge jump and land up to 100 feet (30.5 metres) beyond the jump! The racetrack is designed to challenge the driver's skill and the maneuverabilty of the sled.

In snocross the drivers race against one another, with the driver getting the holeshot, or first off the start line, gaining an important advantage in the race to the first tight corner. While drivers' snowmobiles may end up tangled with one another, or tipped onto their sides, during the frantic first seconds of the event, the race continues. Racetrack corner officials

In snocross racing a long flat tabletop is usually erected directly in front of the stands, where promoters expect to have the most concentrated group of spectators. Advertisers and sponsors use various methods to display their products. Here, this driver is making a jump that reaches the top of the fourth sheet of plywood billboards, showing just how high he really is in the air.

Michael Island of Barrie, Ontario, races the Bud Light Ski-Doo. One of the top drivers in snocross, he took the Gold Medal in snocross at the 2004 X Games. Island's go-for-broke, high risk/reward riding style leads to both strong finishes and big crashes. Slight but strong, he has a gift for holding onto his Mod sled on rough tracks. In a regular WPSA Snocross national, main events are usually 15 laps, while the X Games runs a six-lap final, making it more difficult for a rider to come back from a bad start, which proves to be an advantage for the driver getting the holeshot as Island did.

and flagmen are able to help the drivers right their sleds, start them, and get back into the race.

Rules and classes are established with the goal of keeping competition safe and fair. In these extreme snow sporting events drivers are restricted by their ages and skill levels, while the snowmobiles are ranked by engine size and whether they are modified or stock. A modified snowmobile may have qualifying changes made to engines, chassis, suspension, or combinations of all three. Racers run a specified number of laps, with the first one to get the checkered flag declared the winner. Snocross snowmobiles can go from 0 to 70 mph (112 kph) in less than 4 seconds in the top classes. Although capable of topping 110 mph (176 kph), snocross sleds rarely hit 55 mph (88 kph) because of the tight track design. Drivers rely on quick bursts of power instead of high speed.

The Winter X Games added a HillCross event to their program in 2001. X Games HillCross is similar to SnoCross and is participated in by many of the same drivers. The HillCross competition sets six rac-

ers up against each other in a head-to-head race to see who can cross the finish line first. However, instead of going down the hill on a snowboard or skis, competitors race up the hill on a snowmobile. Tearing it up on the Skier X course, anything can happen as the racers try to reach the top at the fastest speed.

A hill climb racing event is different from a Hill-Cross in that hill climbs do not have one to one competition. In a hill climb the course must consist of an ice or snow incline, free of obstructions that might cause an unsafe situation. Depending on regional variations there may be marked portions of the course for drivers to maneuver at the lowest reaches of the hill or mountain. Each driver takes an independent run at the hill, with a required loop at the top of the run to return back to the staging area at the bottom. The driver's highmark (point furthest up the hill) is measured by a transit (tool used to determine grades and elevations) or by the eye levels of race personnel on the side of the course. Like snocross, hill climb racers are divided by age, level of skill, and the type of snowmobile they are riding.

The final type of extreme racing on snow still participated in by drivers is cross-country or cross country racing. This type of event varies, depending on

These snocross drivers are racing for year-end top placings in the RMXCRC (Rocky Mountain Cross Country Racing Circuit) as well as race day payback in West Yellowstone, Montana, so it's throttle down through the first corner.

the location, but there are minimum standards that must be met to be a sanctioned cross-country race event. These include: the course is primarily on land following a defined or marked course; the course may be looped in an area at least three miles long; the total distance must have 25 miles (40 km) or more. The classes are generally established by the type of machine entered.

The newest development for extreme snow sports lovers is the Freestyle event. While this is a judged competition, rather than a racing event, the flips and turns astound spectators. The IFSA (International Freestyle Snocross Association) sanctions exhibitions to ensure the safety of participants and promote the sport. Freestyle drivers use their sleds to perform aerial demonstrations such as the back flip, bar hop, cat walk, and others.

Usually a panel of IFSA judges, between two and five members, is assigned to judge each event. A score is given from each judge, ranging from 0-100 points with 100 being the best possible run. At the end of each run the judges' scores are added and averaged, giving the rider a score from 0-100 for the run. Rid-

These two racers are being staged, or lined up at the starting line, waiting their turn to take a run at Snow King Mountain in Jackson Hole, Wyoming, for the World Championship Hill Climb. The original racecourse in 1976 was located above what is now Snow King Resort and only went a short distance up the hill. Thirty-six drivers from the Jackson Hole Snow Devil members and the Pinedale, Wyoming, snowmobile club, entered.

Snocross racing is all about testing metal—that of the driver as well as the machine. This snocross racer raises his arm in victory as he takes the win in one of his heat races at the Duluth National Snocross race in November of 2005. Duluth has been ranked among the top ten outdoor towns in the United States.

ers are judged on their style, the degree of difficulty of the move, continuity, amplitude, and originality. Each individual judge's score is based on the following: 50% towards the number of tricks along with the consistency and timing of those tricks in a single run, 20% to the showmanship of the run, and 30% to the degree of difficulty of the tricks performed during the run. While the sport is in its infancy it draws a lot of spectators wherever it is featured.

Driver Rules

Rules for drivers are established by individual governing bodies, affiliates, or associations, with the International Snowmobile Racing, Inc. (ISR) rules providing the standard. This non-profit group is based in West Bend, Wisconsin. The rules begin with the age and qualifications of the individual in snocross, which is the only one of these extreme snow events encouraging the participation of young drivers. By WPSA, and its regional organizations' rules, children under the age of 10 are only allowed to participate in the 120 classes. There are also three classes of juniors: Juniors 10–13, Juniors 14–15, and Juniors 16–17. Boys and girls generally race against one another in the youngest classes.

The 120 classes are: 120 Stock for ages 4 to 7 (up to 12 mph or 19 kph); 120 Stock 8 to 12 (up to 18 mph or 29 kph); and 120 Champ ages 6 to 12. These young racers learn the rules they'll need to participate in snowmobile racing as they grow older.

Drivers who are 13 years of age may advance from Juniors to sport classes or semi-pro classes, however they must be 16 to enter a pro class. All drivers can only race in one level. Regulations are in place to govern when a driver must advance to the next level of experience and ability through the sport, semi-pro, and pro classes. Other classes offered in various locations on the regional circuits include: Novice (beginner), Women's stock, Women's Plus 25 (25 years of age and older), Pro Women, and Pro Plus 35 (35 years of age and older).

The machines allowed in the classes help ensure safe events, so that the younger, less-experienced drivers are the most limited in the type of machine they may ride. As the drivers gain expertise they may move up to faster sleds until they reach the fastest class, the Pro Open. Pro Open machines are up to 600 cc liquid cooled engines.

All drivers need to wear safety equipment on the racetrack. The most important is a snell-approved full-face helmet, which must be securely fastened and worn even in the tune-up area. Helmets are required to be 75% blaze orange in color, so that drivers can be easily identified in snow dust on the track. Blaze or-

This Hall of Fame sled is the original 1978 Ski-Doo RV Cross Country racing sled driven by Gerard Karpik. Until the development of this model by Ski-Doo, Polaris snowmobiles dominated the sport of cross-country racing. When he started his winning streak Karpik was 24 years old—a construction worker from Eveleth, Minnesota. The RV came equipped with a 340 free air engine, 15-inch track, and a 34-inch ski stance, which made it six inches wider than the rest of the 1978 Ski-Doo line.

Jonny Hentges, a Semi-Pro racer out of Shakopee, Minnesota, comes over the hill ready to take his Polaris over the last moguls in a fight to the finish against an opposing Ski-Doo, to the checkered flag.

ange must also cover a specified portion of the driver's back and front, along with upper body protection and shoulder pads for both snocross and cross-country racing. A racing vest is required, since motocross vests or hockey equipment do not meet the rules standards. Other mandatory items include: gloves, appropriate clothing, at least above ankle leather boots, shin and knee guards that cover from the instep to above the knee, and elbow pads are highly recommended. Eye protection is mandatory. Once dressed, the final thing the driver must wear is a racing bib or other form of garment marked with their issued number.

Snowmobile Rules

The snowmobile rules begin with identification procedures to ensure each driver is scored correctly in events. All sleds must be marked with the driver's racing number, which must adhere to the size and width required by current regulations. Both sides of the machine must display the number in order to be scored. Pro drivers must also have their machine number on the windshield of the sled.

Sled safety rules are some of the most important ones enforced. All machines must have a safety switch or secondary kill switch on the right side of the handlebar, which will stop the machine's engine. Tether switches are also required, so that when the driver is dislodged from his sled the machine stops immediately.

All machines must use warm-up stands when the rear of the sled is raised to clean out the engine, or the track, in the pit or paddock area at all times. The warm up stand must meet specifications, so that it will stop anything that might be thrown from the moving track. Side extensions on the stands are also mandatory to ensure the safety of everyone in the area.

The rules governing the machines and what modifications may or may not be allowed for the different classes are established annually by the ISR or International Snowmobile Racing organization, which puts out an annual ISR Snowmobile Racing Yearbook of the rules. The ISR is located in West Bend, Wisconsin.

The pit or paddock area (used for equipment parking and fine-tuning of sleds) gives spectators who buy a pit pass a look at what happens behind the scenes at a race. This pit area has the Arctic Cat factory racers and teams all working out of their racing semis. The number 3 sled, in the foreground of the photo, is driven by factory pro driver Shaun Crapo. The race semis are equipped with enough tools and parts to repair a broken or damaged sled between races, so the drivers don't lose any track time or points at a race.

The Evolution of Extreme Snow Sports

Snowmobile racing on snow began with some of the most extreme challenges against the elements that men, or women, have ever undertaken. Edgar Hetteen, Erling Falk, along with Rudy and Bessie Billberg crossed Alaska with Polaris Sno-Travelers in March of 1960. It was, for Hetteen, a way to prove the potential for the snowmobile—and ultimately he hoped, to reach customers around the world.

Hetteen's journey took twenty-one days and 1200 miles (1920 km) from Bethel on the Bering Sea, across the wilderness. His board of directors had declared the idea was a huge folly—a tremendously stupid one, but he persisted anyway. Leaving with three

Sno-Travelers, the group braved blizzards, torrential winds, and even sandstorms, until they reached Fairbanks. The media caught the story and ran with it, spreading the story around the globe, but for Hetteen and his board, it caused the final break and he left Polaris.

Ralph Plaisted's journeys also astonished the world. His first, in 1965, set a time and distance record for snow travel: 200 miles (320 km) from Ely to St. Paul, Minnesota in 13 hours and 52 minutes, battling temperatures of −41 degrees. But that trip only gave Plaisted a taste for more.

After a failed expedition in 1966, Plaisted achieved his dream to snowmobile to the North Pole in 1968.

Drivers get a victory lap carrying the checkered flag after the final race of a class at many events. The crowd in this race may look a little odd, as this West Yellowstone RMXCHC snocross event ran in 60-degree temperatures, so spectators are in their shirtsleeves instead of parkas. The driver, however, is wearing all of the required equipment, which you can see from the helmet and racing bib displaying his number.

These three youngsters are entering the track to line up for the 120 class event to run. The 120s start on the tabletop in front of the crowd, rather than the usual entry point onto the track. A track official often walks in front of the youngest class of drivers to lead them up to the start flag and get them lined up. The snowmobiles make one or more complete laps during the race, with quite a few of the young drivers getting "air" with their minis as they take the same jumps as their parents do in the adult classes.

He, along with Jean-Luc Bombardier (J. Armand's nephew), Gerry Pitzl, and Walt Pederson, set out with four Super Olympic 300 cc Ski-Doos on March 7, 1968. Forty-three days, two hours, and thirty minutes later, on April 19, 1968, their location at the geographical North Pole was confirmed by U.S. Air Force planes. The trip had taken them 825 miles (1330 km) across the Arctic.

While it's hard to define the moment organized competitions began on the snow, one of the earliest was sponsored by the Hodag Sportsman's club at its annual ice fishing Jamboree in January of 1961. Five Ski-Doos raced at speeds close to 30 mph (48 kph) over the snow and iced-over surface of Boom Lake near Rhinelander, Wisconsin, with more than a thousand spectators on hand to see what would happen.

Spectators were in for a surprise at the Lac LaRonge, Saskatchewan races in March of 1962. Polaris Sno-Travelers raced two miles over the tips of evergreen trees through deep, untouched snow, competing against each other and dog teams. The rules required that everyone had to break trail, just like real trappers in the North, so it proved the performance of the snowmobile in this terrain. It was an easy victory for the snowmobiles.

Once snowmobiles had been easily proven to beat dog teams, the challenge moved to sled against sled. December of 1963 featured the first true cross-country snowmobile only race on a designed course in Marquette, Michigan. The machines sped over small hills, and like modern snocross, across a field of man-made banked turns and three-foot-high ramps. Drivers and spectators all enjoyed the thrills.

St. Paul, Minnesota, which soon grew into one of the most well-known venues for cross-country racing with its International 500 or I-500, held its first race on January 25, 1964, in Phalen Park. Forty contestants sped over a rolling course along the lakeshore, hitting speeds of more than 35 miles per hour (56 kph) on a hard-packed four-inch snow base. The first Winnipeg to St. Paul International cross-country race was held in 1966, getting lots of media attention in both countries.

The weekend after St. Paul's first race in 1964, the first International Motorized Ski Sled Races were held in Lancaster, New Hampshire. Forty sleds, all

These two drivers have just crossed the finish line—notice the Race Director holding the checkered flag on the edge of the track. The Ski-Doo sled has taken first place by just a few feet over Moreau on his Polaris. Drivers are required to have their sled numbers displayed on both sides of the machines, so track officials (along with spectators) can readily identify them.

Ski-Doos, raced across a five-mile cross-country course that had been laid out by a Muskeg tractor. One of the most significant things that happened at this race was organizers trying to equalize the competition by adding sand-filled saddlebags to the sleds of light drivers, so every machine had an equal weight to carry. It was the beginning of rules that would try to ensure fair competition for decades to come.

One week later, the Eagle River World Championship Snowmobile Derby (title officially registered in 1966) in Eagle River, Wisconsin, the racing event that sent snowmobile competition into an upward spiral that spun almost out of control for a decade, was first held February 9, 1964. With the first broad media coverage the race drew more than 5,000 spectators that first year to view an array of races. These included: ski joring (skiing behind a snowmobile), hill climbing, and cross-country obstacle races. The event also set a precedent by drawing participants with experimental models from the factories: Roger Skime from Arctic Cat, and Stan Hayes on Polaris.

At the end of the race there was plenty more discussion about what should be allowed in a race— Roger Skime's Arctic was challenged with a protest, but he was cleared of the charge of using a special fuel. Other controversies abounded. It was the start of a rules debate that seemed never-ending.

February 28, 1964, the Kawartha Lakes Tourist Association brought together the first cooperative Canadian-American race. Called the Kawartha

These two Strandlund racing team Polaris sleds give you a close up view of how a snocross sled is set-up for a race. Snowmobile design has changed dramatically over the years from the first "peg leg" or leaf sprung snowmobiles, to the modern sleds with independent front suspension. Early cross-country riders were jarred by every bump on the course, while today's drivers can thank technology for the ability to ride today's cross-country, snocross, and hill climb events.

Earl Reimer rides both the Pro classes and the Pro Veteran or Pro Plus 35 class with the Blair Morgan Racing Team. Riding out of Waldhof, Ontario, Reimer has been racing since 1975, so is one of the most experienced drivers on the track. He has competed in the X Games as well as following the WPSA circuit, using Arctic Cat, Polaris, and Ski-Doo snowmobiles at different points in his career. His nickname is "Scrap Iron."

Cup, the first race featured cross-country and closed-course racing. With the snowmobile industry booming there were new brands in addition to the three already established: Snow Cruiser, Hus-Ski, Fox Trac, Outboard Marine Corporation (OMC), and Moto-ski. Snowmobile racing fever was starting to grow. Peterborough is still host to the National Kawartha Cup Pro Snowcross race in 2006.

Snowmobile manufacturers jumped in enthusiastically for the first Hodag Cross-Country Snowmobile Marathon, sending the best drivers and the newest models to prove their metal. The race started in Rhinelander, Wisconsin, ran through Three Lakes, and ended on Main Street in Eagle River. Of the 110 entries only 22 failed to finish—many of those rested against tree stumps or other sleds they'd

run into. The Hodag ran February 6, 1965 and the Eagle River race the next day.

Eagle River was also the organizational grounds of the first large historical snowmobile sanctioning body—the United States Snowmobile Association. [USSA] Dan Satran, an Eagle River newspaper publisher, called a meeting in the spring of 1965 to discuss the issue of creating a standardized set of rules. Ten Eagle River businessmen each contributed $100 to get the organization off the ground, electing Satran as president, and Peter Anderson as treasurer. Its first public meetings addressed structure and recreational concerns. It took nearly two years, until April of 1967, for a board to sit down to discuss the first comprehensive racing rules, in Minneapolis, Minnesota.

These drivers are suiting up for some hot laps in the pit or paddock area with their Polaris sleds. Driver #999, is in front of his sled, which is positioned on the mandatory stand for safety. Notice the stand's side flaps, which will protect everyone in the pit area from flying debris when the machine is revved and the track spins. This driver is wearing the required equipment, including his racing number, which is part of the design of his racing gear.

The first snowmobile race sanctioning body to be organized and functioning in North America was founded by the Alaska Snowmobile Dealers and Distributors Association [ASDDA] in November of 1965. Alaskan races included cross-country and other events. Machine classifications were based on a formula that took weight and horsepower into consideration.

It comes as no surprise that Alaska became home to some of the most treacherous and challenging cross-country snowmobile races ever held. The first was held as part of the Anchorage Fur Rendezvous in January of 1966. Marv Dickerson, riding a Johnson, won with a time of one hour, five minutes, 32 seconds. Allan Smith of Mountain View took the victory that March in an event called the all-Alaska Snowmobile Championship, which scored points over the course of a seven-day event.

The year 1966 also marked the beginning of racing in West Yellowstone, a tradition still in place. The West Yellowstone Roundup was held March 17-19, and not only proved to be the establishment of a central point for snowmobile racing in the west, but also the birth of the Western Snowmobile Association, which was just one of a dozen or more new snowmobile organizations. Soft powder made the first cross-country course one of the most interesting—and changeable—tracks in the country. Snowmobiles pounding over the course soon had the snow packed into gullies and holes, often as deep as 8 or 10 feet (2.4 to 3 meters) that caught unwary drivers and their machines. Today, West Yellowstone holds its World Snowmobile Expo each March at the close of the snocross racing season.

In 1967 Duluth, Minnesota, joined the ranks of communities destined to play a part in snowmobile racing for decades to come. Their second Christmas City of the North Indoor Snowmobile races launched the 1967-1968 racing season. The arena, of course, was filled with smoke, so while spectators didn't have to worry about the cold, they certainly got a true "taste" of racing watching the 340 feet (104 metres) long banked oval track. But bigger things were yet to come with Duluth's racing program.

Prizes kept pace with the frenzy for racing. The 1968 winner of the Hodag was guaranteed not only a cash purse, but also a brand new shiny Javelin automobile! With so much at stake a dispute arose, which after a bitterly contested debate, eventually had the prize awarded to Bob Eastman. But as the stakes grew higher and higher, individuals and teams often found ways to make their sleds go faster that weren't necessarily by the spirit of the rules. A well-circulated saying was, "There's cheaters, and then there's losers."

Drivers and manufacturers through the country looked for ways to prove their machines, right down in to the Nevada Mountains on the Nevada-California border. Mountain racing was the wild new event. Mammoth Lakes, California, held a race in 1968 that started from the bottom of the mountain and ran to the top—however the driver could get there. A smoke bomb at the top took the place of a flagman and the sleds roared up the mountain when it exploded. Many of the same drivers also competed at Park City, Utah, running side by side up the mountain trail. The sports of hill climbing and hillcross had been born.

Cross-country racing was important to manufacturers through the next decade. The 1976–1977 season was the year of the Deere, with John Deere Liquidators totally dominating the sport by taking five of the eight major races, finishing up in second in the other three. But glory has a limited time span in snowmobile racing and Gerard Karpik or "King Karpik" as he was soon known, rode the Ski-Doo Cross Country RV to fame and fortune for an unprecedented four in a row win record by a single driver, and a top five finish in the 1978 season. The next year was even better for Karpik, with a High-Point title and Ski-Doo's first cross-country championship, which he repeated in 1980.

Everyone was still pursuing snowmobile racing to the extreme. Still running today, the Tesoro Iron Dog is the longest, toughest cross-country snowmobile race in the world. First ran in 1984 over a

This Polaris sled is in staging waiting to be called for its race. Notice the front-end design of the sled, which illustrates the improvements in suspension since the original cross-country racers of the 1960s and 1970s were manufactured. These changes are what make modern sleds tough enough to take the torture of a snocross track. Drivers also use more aggressive ski profiles than ones used by snowmobile trail riders, so that once the sled is on the snow surface they can quickly maneuver to get around another driver or find a faster line.

distance of 1,009 miles (1615 km) from Wasilla to Nome, the mileage and number of days has changed over the years. By 2005 the course ran 2,018 miles, taking three days, from Wasilla to Nome, and back to Wasilla. Teams of two drivers, each on their own sled, compete. The 2005 event was won by Marc McKenna and Nick Olstad, on Arctic Cats, with a time of 52:59. Some years alternate, running Wasilla, Nome, to Fairbanks.

In March, 1979, the USSA sanctioned its first snocross race, modeled on motorcycle motocross racing. It was the Sunday feature at the newly coined Ya-Hoo days in West Yellowstone. Constructed in the city park, the track was a twisting, winding, banked course that started with a short straightaway to a

You can see these three Ski-Doo drivers are kicking up a lot of swirling snow dust with their spinning tracks. While the driver up front may have good visibility, it rapidly diminishes for those close enough to be challenging the first place driver. Race numbers, as you can see, are important in identifying drivers, since their suits and helmets are all very similar.

Jesse West, Arctic Cat driver #888, started racing snocross in 2002. He hails out of Thief River Falls, Minnesota, home of the Arctic Cat factory. Right now he's just half a sled length ahead of another Semi-Pro racer. A driver needs to be at least 16 years of age and have qualified through the standard advancement procedures in order to move to Pro classes.

jump. It only took an hour to run the whole race, which mostly consisted of local drivers, but the crowd wasn't ready to go home—so, like all good performers should, the drivers came out and did some individual time trials for an encore.

It was the beginning of something big, and snocross races began to spring up everywhere as the new decade of the 1980s began, with the Dayco Holiday Spectacular in Alexandria, Minnesota, making a feature presentation. The pre-Christmas event invited all of the manufacturers' top drivers to race a course laid out over the snow. European racers had been competing on the tight corners, banked turns, and short bumps since the early 1970s, so the promoters had their tracks to use as a model.

Promoters convinced manufacturers to participate by billing the event as the final proving ground for best handling and most durable sleds consumers could buy. All eight manufacturers were invited to send three drivers each: Moto-Ski, Arctic Cat, Scorpion, Yamaha, Arctic Cat, Ski-Doo, John Deere, and Kawasaki. Larry Coltom, on an Arctic Cat, emerged victorious from the round robin event. While already retired, he'd built a practice track and done his homework before jumping on board the new Arctic Cat El Tigre 6000.

It didn't take promoters long to figure out that snocross was a lot more appealing to crowds than cross-country racing, even if the obstacles were similar. With a track right in front of them, and often, great sports facilities behind them, they had the best this competitive sport could offer. Plus, by keeping the rules to stock machines it opened up a whole new low-cost format for local racers—just like racing had been in the beginning. Early snocross events sometimes used an ice lemans course, which is also a modern form of ice racing.

However, even with all the pluses, it took awhile for snocross or ice lemans to catch on across the country due to the usual racing glitches of rules and what kinds of machines would run. By the 1983-1984 season there were snocross circuits across the snow belt and lots of races through the United States and Canada. Driver, Guy Useldinger, had the unofficial title of "Mr. Snocross" after making the move from cross-country racing. He'd won in Sweden in 1979 at an International Class competition, and helped introduce the snocross concept to the United States. In 1988, the Quadna snocross (a ski resort in Hill City, Minnesota) had a record 270 entries and a variety of classes. The next breakthrough at Quadna was the 1990 addition of a Women's class.

The evolution of the sport, also billed as super-cross, continued with various influences from within the industry. Duluth, Minnesota, involved in racing since the beginning, made some adjustments to their program in 1992—this one took place on Spirit Mountain. Its success made the industry sit back and re-evaluate what the crowd was looking for. While many snocross events so far had been on lakes, using a lemans course, Spirit Mountain's natural terrain drew much bigger crowds: 15,000 people over three days in its second year, a number double that of the first! The race also drew 508 driver entries, so it didn't take much imagination to figure out that everybody enjoyed the big jumps and berms.

By the end of the 1990s the World Series of Snocross added a Womens Pro Am class, officially recognizing women as professional drivers, rather than the "powder puff" variety of races that had prevailed historically. The addition of snocross to the X Games in

These two Polaris sleds are racing head-to-head in a situation that occurs on any kind of extreme snow racing course from cross-country to hillcross to snocross. The reduced visibility comes from a few things: snowdust from sleds at the front of the pack as well as an overcast day with light snow flurries. Racers in the early days didn't have the advantage these drivers do of goggles with special fog cutter impregnated lenses and foam filter vents to keep out snowdust.

Competition is keen in this photo—the two snocross drivers are so close at first glance it appears the two tracks belong to one sled in the lead! Notice the clear sky along with the amount of snow kicked up by those spinning tracks and you can image how much more challenging it is for the two oncoming drivers you can see coming over the hill. The flagmen, standing on the top of the hill, is attentive to the action, ready to bring out the yellow flag if one of the sleds has any kind of problem.

The Duluth National racecourse features a North series of spectator stands that provide a whole view from above, of the drivers taking the bumps. Here, you can see drivers as they increase their speed down the straight part of the course trying to overtake the sleds in front. You'll see drivers all across the track taking the moguls, as each looks for the line that will get him past the sled in front.

1998 recognized its place in the world of worldwide extreme winter competition.

Hill climbs, meanwhile, took off in the Western areas of North America, with the creation of the Rocky Mountain Snowmobile Hill climb Association [RMSHA] and the British Columbia Snowmobile Federation's hill climb circuit, in the mid 1990s. By 1997 joint efforts allowed members to compete with both for the prize money, which was big! Average payback at RMSHA events was $20,000 to $25,000.

The granddaddy of hill climbs, and the longest running event of this part of the sport, is the annual Jackson Hole World Championship Hill Climb. Running since 1976, the event is scheduled at the end of the skiing season so the sleds can use Snow King Mountain, which rises 1,500 vertical feet above the town of Jackson, Wyoming. The hill climb course follows a route that, near the summit, steepens to nearly a 45-degree angle. Hill climbers who lose it on the upper reaches of the course often tumble hundreds of feet back downhill.

The King of the Hill title went to "King Kirk" Williamson on his Mach I Ski-Doo for his second consecutive championship in March 1997 at the Jackson Hole Hill climb. Just as exciting, he got to bank the more than $10,000 in prize and contingency cash. The win also cinched him a spot in the *Snow Week* Top 10 Racers of the Year. Earlier, in the 1990–1991 season, Kim Ropelato was the first hill climb competitor to ever make the list.

Snocross racers captured quite a few of the top ten positions from *Snow Week* that year. "Captain Kirk" Hibbert, the 39 year-old legend of the sport, finished the season as the Pro 440 points champion in the ISOC association—for the fifth consecutive year. Toni Haikonen captured quite a few wins and a few scars along with his *Snow Week* Top Ten award. At MRP Muskegon he finished second in Open and third in the 600 class, but had his leg ripped open by the studs on his sled during a crash. Forty stitches later he didn't even slow down, but had them pull out while he was grabbing a second place victory at the ISOC Canterbury race a week later. Winner of the Eagle River World Championship snocross event on his Yamaha, Chris Vincent also made it onto the top 10.

The year 1997 also marked the beginning of an era—the era of the Superman of Snocross—Blair Morgan, out of Prince Albert, Saskatchewan, hit the moguls. *Snow Week* named him Rookie of the Year after his first race in the United States at the MRP West Yellowstone event. He'd spent the earlier part of the season in the Canadian Northstar Racing Association, then the U.S. race took him right to the top as he beat out some of the best snocross racers in the world to finish second to Kirk Hibbert in the feature.

Following on the success of the Hibbert drivers, Kirk and son Tucker, at the 2000 X Games—Kirk was the oldest driver to compete in snocross, and Tucker the youngest, at 15, to ever win a Gold medal—the 2000–2001 snocross season was truly wild!

Brad Pitlik, sponsored by Ski-Doo, is from Eagle River, Wisconsin. One of his career wins includes the Eagle River 24 Hour Endurance Race, which uses a LeMans-style course. Pitlik races WPSA Pro classes for the Kowalski Racing Team out of Whitewater, Wisconsin.

Tucker won 12 of 22 WSA (World Snowmobile Association) events and claimed the Pro Open season points title in a duel that lasted the whole year against Blair Morgan. Morgan, however, snatched the 2001 X Games gold from Tucker.

Blair Morgan and Tucker Hibbert continued to be the duelling duo until Hibbert retired from the snocross circuit to pursue motocross, with his only foray into snocross annually to compete in the X Games. When the 2005 WSA Lake Geneva series final event rolled around on March 18–20, the year end high point totals went to Steve Martin on his Ski-Doo in the Pro Open, and T.J. Gulla on his Polaris in Pro Stock. It was the first time since 1998 that any Snocross pro title had gone to anyone but Blair Morgan or Tucker Hibbert. Morgan had been taken out of the competition right after the X Games with a broken leg during a race.

Pro Women's snocross racing competition was also tense for the 2004–2005 season. Victoria Hawley hit Lake Geneva with a slim lead over the 2000 High point winner Julie Thul, so everyone knew it would be a fight to the finish. With Amanda Wolfe and Sarah McQuestion right in the thick of the battle, Thul eventually pulled up front to take the lead and the season's victory.

At the season's end four top snocross drivers were recognized on the 2005 *Snow Week* Top 10 Racers List. They included Blair Morgan, Steve Martin, Robbie Malinoski, and D.J. Eckstrom. Morgan and Malinoski are both Canadians, from Saskatchewan, while Martin is from Wyoming, and Eckstrom hails from Minnesota.

Hill climb extreme snow driver, Jason Crane from Idaho, also made the *Snow Week* List. Crane had an impressive season, with two class wins and a third-place finish at the World Championship Hill climb in Jackson Hole, along with a strong season. RMSHA were the sanctioning organization at the World Championship in Jackson Hole, from which Vincent (Vinnie) Clark emerged as King of the Hill on his Ski-Doo. It was a challenging year on the hill, as it was icy and compact on the lower portion, while on the face of the Upper Exhibition the snow was wet and heavy—the hill often won and the snowmobiles lost traction. Many riders settled for a highmark, while a few were able to crest the hill and record a time. Winners emerged on all three competing brands: Ski-Doo, Polaris, and Arctic Cat.

Women were right out there too in the 2004–2005 United States Cross Country (USCC) circuit, with Jenna Sobeck, a newcomer, taking the Women's class at the Munising 300 in Michigan on March 18–19. The largest event on the USCC schedule and the first cross-country race in the Upper Peninsula for many years, it drew 114 driver entries. Bryan Dyrdahl won

A forklift is used to remove damaged or not running machines from the track. Snowmobiles are pulled to the side of the racecourse by flag-men and track officials when this occurs, but not removed until the event has completely finished. The next class is held at the start line until the forklift can take the machine off the track, then back to the owner's trailer in the pits, so repairs can begin immediately for the next event.

the Pro Open event, his second victory of the season. It wasn't enough, however, to edge out Polaris rider, Corey Davidson, who took his third consecutive USCC season points title as the season wrapped up.

As the 2005–2006 season began for extreme snow racers, some new rules came down from the ISR. Snocross drivers faced a new rule that dropped the engine limit on Open sleds from 800 cc down to 600 cc, so mechanics and drivers had lots of changes to make. Another change, which pleased everyone, was the removal of the restriction that shock absorbers used on sleds had to be the same length as the originals—the new ruling allowed teams to run shocks of any length. The WPSA, also changing to meet the needs of the racing world, looked forward to a full season of exciting race coverage through ESPN II. Extreme snow sports continued to grow and evolve.

Memorable Moments in Extreme Snow Events

There has been a continual debate over factory involvement in the sport of snowmobile racing, with various options tried over the years to reach a happy medium that satisfied everyone: sponsors, spectators, factories, and independent racers. For the 1971–1972 racing season Polaris proposed a challenge in which the factories would all participate on the same slate of races, instead of dispatching their drivers across the snow zone. The head-to-head competition would, presumably, show consumers which machines excelled in which venues.

The Winnipeg to St. Paul International 500 Cross Country Race was on the Polaris list of challenges, so the Can-Am team, with DuHamel as the key driver, set off for Winnipeg to compete against the other factories on Ski-Doo's behalf. The cross-country racers didn't consider DuHamel much of a worry, since it was a well known fact he'd gone directly from the motocross track to the snowmobile oval track, without the break-in learning period they'd all put in on cross-country driving and racing. Six hundred miles took a lot more than the 15 minutes an oval driver was used to. Cross-country racing not only took a different style of riding, it meant a different kind of snowmobile set-up and race strategy.

Dorothy Mercer, while she'd earned a lot of respect for her skill on the track, was another entrant who

The snocross track is built by molding snow, either natural or artificial, to create the moguls or bumps, along with the tabletop, tight turns and corners that make up the course. The machine is a groomer that has a blade in the front to move snow, while the rear is used to smooth the snow out once it has been pushed into place. It takes many hours to build the course initially, plus the groomer comes out on the track off and on through the course of an event to keep the track in peak condition.

was far from the list of favorites even though she was on the Polaris factory team—in fact she is the only woman in history to race with a factory. The year before she'd started 270th and finished in 16th place, but still, lots of the men had dropped out due to mechanical or other problems. Everyone knew Mercer was tough, after all she was a 29-year-old championship skier, rodeo bronc rider, and motorcycle jockey and she was ready for a run at the men's classes. She had already set and re-set the women's world snowmobile speed record and was ready to give the guys a run for their money over the long haul.

The landscape of the first couple of hundred miles of the course was as flat and white as a fresh-made hospital bed. While the constant wind worked its way through visors, stinging faces, the biggest challenge was the effect it had on the snow. There is no soft powder on the prairies. Even falling snow loses that innocent quality the instant the wind hurls it at a

fencepost and it drops, stunned, into the fill dirt and snowdrifts. Ditches are full of white cement, sculpted and re-sculpted on a daily basis.

Regardless of the type of suspension the snowmobile has, it's plain rough to be a ditch rider, and that's what a lot of the Winnipeg to Minneapolis race was. Each landing connected a rider's tailbone with the frozen lump of foam that passed for a seat. As long as their strength held, riders could keep their chins above the handlebars, instead of kissing them with each wild bump. Riding on this kind of snow, riders don't hang on with their arms for long unless they're Superman. They use their legs, riding each snowdrift like it's a rodeo bronc. Luckily, by the time the eight seconds are up, the riders have moved onto another bank with a different kind of buck. And this is where Dorothy Mercer's background came into play.

Mercer crashed during the first day, not far out of Winnipeg—but that was inevitable at the speeds she

This photo has six sleds all vying for the coveted first place position out of the first corner. The ski-doos, on the left side, are up on the berm or the wall of snow that is built up in the corner by the spinning tracks of the sleds on the lower areas. While the track changes with each lap, drivers will often pick out a line, or place on the course, that seems to be the fastest for their machine set-up and driving style. The Parts Unlimited marker helps drivers identify the track edge in snowdust.

was running. Picking herself up, she climbed right back onto the sled and roared on. The next day she tangled with a barbed wire fence and had to cut herself free. It was, unfortunately, one of the hazards of cross-country driving. Then, like a few other drivers, she ran out of gas, flipped a few more times, got up, checked for major injuries, and kept on going.

By the first day out, 137 sleds and drivers broke down or took too hard of a crash to continue before they pulled into the stop at Crookston. Leroy Lindblad, the favorite, was out. By day two, Jim Bernat was done, and Bob Eastman went on the third. By St. Cloud, Minnesota, Mercer was up to sixth in the race—and DuHamel was just ahead of her.

The cheering crowd at the finish line in St. Paul

didn't know what to expect—their favorites had all been eliminated except for Wes Pesek. Seeing a Polaris wasn't a surprise, but when Dorothy Mercer flipped her visor and they realized who had made it first to the checkered flags, they were more than a little shocked! Mercer set the fastest time of the day and broke the record for the final leg, but was only third in overall time. Her cross-country record time still stands today for women.

Yvon DuHamel came up with the winning time to earn the cross-country title on his debut race. It was the first and only time Ski-Doo ever won the Winnipeg race. DuHamel was also the only driver to win the Eagle River World Championship oval race, along with a prestigious cross-country title.

You can see nine sleds coming directly at you down this spectator side of the track in West Yellowstone, Montana. The front sleds are already in the air after coming up over the bumps or moguls, with a couple of them getting ready to take a tight line in the upcoming corner. The shallower bumps here are closer to what a cross-country racer would have encountered decades ago on a natural track over fields and roadways.

Extreme Women Racers on the Snow

While the majority of extreme snow racers have always been men, a few women have left their mark on the sport as well.

• The first major purse won by a female driver was $1,000 in the first Alaska State Women's Championship cross-country race in 1969. The winner was Beverly Dugan, one of only 28 to finish the 100-mile event.

• Dorothy Mercer set a Women's Record in 1972 for cross-country racing that still stands, taking third place in the prestigious Winnipeg to St. Paul International 500 race. She also set several consecutive speed run records, with the highest being 138.7 mph (222 kph) on the Polaris X-3 in 1973.

• Kathy Nedrow won the first USSA Woman Driver of the Year Award in 1974.

• Dianne Miller was the first woman to compete in a SnoPro event and the first woman to race the Soo I-500. After dominating the women's classes and showing well in the men's, she earned the overall Driver of the Year points competition on the MISA circuit in 1975.

• Roxann Steinke was the first woman to win a traditionally all-men's class in the 1976 St. Paul's World Series. She beat Mike Decker to the checkered flag to take the Mod-Stock 340 class.

• Shilah Dalebout became the first female to conquer the Upper Exhibition in Jackson Hole History Hillclimb in 2005.

Chris Kafka, sled #991, is a Polaris driver from Stratford, Wisconsin. Competing in the WPSA Pro events, he made his first Pro Final National race when he was just 16. Snowmobile racing is part of a family tradition for him, since his father, Glen Kafka, was a well-known race mechanic.

Who's in the Hall of Fame from Extreme Snow Sports?

Steve Ave – An original inductee in 1988. Raced Ski-Doo.

Bernat, Jim – Inducted in 1991. Polaris.

Bender, Tim – Inducted in 1999. Rode Yamaha and Polaris.

Cormican, Dale – Inducted 1997. Rode Arctic Cat Panthers, John Deere, Polaris, and Ski-Doo.

Decker, Audrey – Inducted in 1989. Rode Ski-Doo.

Donahue, Bobby – Inducted in 1997. Drove Yamaha, Kawasaki, and Ski-Doo.

DuHamel, Yvon – An original inductee in 1988. Rode Ski-Doo.

Eastman, Bob – An original inductee in 1988. Rode Polaris.

Eck, Duane – Inducted in 1990. Rode Ski-Doo, Arctic Cat, and Polaris.

Ewing, Darcy – Inducted 2006. Raced Arctic Cat, Ski-Doo Kawasaki.

Frandsen, Duane – Inducted in 1992. Rode Ski-Doo.

Hayes, Stan – An original inductee in 1988. Rode Mercury and John Deere.

Hulings, Brad – inducted in 1999. Rode Mercury, Polaris, Scorpion, and Ski-Doo.

Janssen, Roger – An original inductee in 1988. Raced Arctic Cat, Chaparral, John Deere, and Polaris.

Karpik, Gerard – Inducted in 1994. Rode Mercury and Ski-Doo.

Linblad, Leroy – Inducted in 1992. Rode Polaris and Ski-Doo.

Lofton, Charlie – Inducted in 1991. Raced Arctic Cat.

Mercer, Dorothy – Inducted in 1993. Raced Polaris.

Muetz, Gordy – Inducted in 2001. Rode Yamaha.

Nelson, Brian – Inducted in 2000. Rode Polaris, Ski-Doo, Arctic Cat, and John Deere.

Rosenquist, Frans - Inducted 2006. Raced Ski-Doo, Sno-Jet, Mercury, Yamaha, Polaris, Kawasaki, Arctic Cat.

Rugland, Larry – Inducted in 1990. Rode Polaris and Ski-Doo.

Struthers, Jack – Inducted in 2004. Rode Polaris.

Thompson, Dave – An original inductee in 1988. Drove Arctic Cat.

Thorsen, Steve – Inducted in 1989. rode Arctic Cat, Polaris, Mercury, Scorpion, and Yamaha.

Trapp, Mike – An original inductee in 1988. Raced Scorpion, Yamaha, and Ski-Doo.

Wicht, John – Inducted in 2003. Rode Kawasaki and Polaris.

EXTREME SNOW SPORT'S AMAZING FACTS:

• The first Winnipeg to St. Paul I-500 cross-country race was run in 1966 and won by Herb Howe.

• The Saf–Jac protective vest that is mandatory for professional snowmobile race drivers was first marketed in the 1974–1975 season. It was developed following a 1974 snowmobile racing accident in which Jacque Knop was killed at Chilton, Wisconsin. Her husband Ken, who also raced, designed and manufactured the jacket, naming it Saf-Jac as a dedication to her. Since 1975 over 10,000 Saf-Jacs have been sold and countless lives saved as a result.

• *Snow Goer* magazine tested the 1975 high performance machines to come up with the following top speed results: Yamaha GPX422 and the Sno*Jet SST F/A 440 topping out at 68 mph (108.8 kph). Close Behind were the Polaris TX 440 (66 mph or 105.6 kph), the Arctic Cat El Tigre 440 (65 mph or 104 kph), the Ski-Doo T'NT FA 440 (63 mph or 100.8 kph). The Rupp Nitro F/A clocked in @ 61 mph (97.6 kph).

• The first International Polar Cup was held in the 1979-1980 season. It included riders from both sides of the Atlantic and was held in Manitoba, Minnesota, Sweden and Finland.

• Feb. 1982 speed tests by *Snow Goer* magazine showed production sled speeds had greatly increased. The Shoot-Out III was won by the Polaris Indy 600 with a top speed of 104.68 mph (167.5 kph). A Ski-doo Blizzard 9700 came in a close second at 102.92mph (164.7 kph) followed by the Kawasaki Interceptor (94.97 mph or 152 kph) and the John Deere Liquifire (87.47 mph or 140 kph).

• January 6, 1982. The experiment into snocross racing received a setback when the opening race put on by the ICCSF attracted only 8 drivers, and about 100 spectators. This was in spite of the excellent preparations made in Hibbing, Minnesota. The poor showing was put down to the postponement of the Central Cross Country lake race at Forest Lake, Minnesota, due to snowstorm. The cross-country race moved to the 6th, the same day, which meant that many drivers, hoping to compete in both races were prevented from doing so. Racing action continued, however, with drivers including Gerard Karpik and Doug Lamm.

• Ward Barnes was the first driver to reach the top of Snow King Mountain at the Jackson Hole Hill climb in 1986.

• In 1991 cross-country racing was very popular in North America, but was considered unique in the Scandinavian countries. In Sweden and Finland, snocross was the race type of choice. There were two professional classes in European snocross, the 56 hp and the open.

• The first stock machine to go "over the top" at the Jackson Hole Hill climb was Mark Thompson on a Ski-Doo Summit 670 in 1996.

• The highest bid item in the *Snow Week* 2001 Auction was $968 for the Tucker Hibbert pants and pullover. The Auction supports grassroots racing.

• Roger Dick, one of the original members of the Polaris Thrill Team, completed the "loop" (a track that made a full circle) during the 2004 Fiftieth Anniversary celebrations of Polaris in Rosseau, Minnesota. It was the first time the Polaris Charger had been used in the stunt since the team was disbanded in 1969 after performing at snowmobile races across the country. Coincidentally, it was Dick's 60th birthday the day of the final demonstration at the Minnesota State Fairgrounds on July 24, 2004.

URLs

World PowerSports Racing Association - **www.wpsaracing.com**
USSA Pro Star Racing Series - **www.ussaprostar.net**
Mountain West Racing Association - **www.mountainwestracing.com**
World Championship Snowmobile Hill Climb – Jackson Hole - **www.snowdevils.org**
SnowRider online magazine - **www.snowridermag.com**
Snowmobile Hall of Fame and Museum - **www.snowmobilehalloffame.com**

In this corner the sleds are making a tight turn, with the Ski-Doo out in front. The Arctic Cat driver has been slowed down through the berm, ending up on the top of the snow and making a wider corner. Notice the driving style of the Ski-Doo driver at this point as the driver stands up on his sled, leaning ahead over his handlebars, and gets on the power coming out of the corner.

West Yellowstone has always been one of the most scenic snocross tracks in North America, as the mountains provide a beautiful backdrop. Here, this driver is airborne, making a double jump on the course. A double is a series of two jumps close enough together for a rider to sail over them and land on the down-side of the second one for the smoothest ride.

Mike Shultz, riding the Polaris sled #5, is from Pillager, Minnesota. He rides the Pro Circuit with the WPSA for a new team, Avalanche Racing. Although injured at an event in Valcourt, Quebec in 2005, he still made the finals in all three of the races he was able to enter in the 2004–2005 season, including the Winter X Games. In the off-season he spends his time with Motocross, mountain biking, and working out at the gym.

This photo was taken in the Snowmobile Hall of Fame Museum. The 1976 John Deere Liquidator 340 was owned and driven by Brian Nelson, who was a two-time winner of the I-500 St. Paul to Winnipeg race. The sled weighed in at 510 pounds (231.8 kg), with a 32-inch (81.3 cm) ski stance. It had a 60 hp liquid cooled engine. Nelson also took first place in the North Dakota Governor's Cup and the Regina to Minot 300 Mile Cross Country Races.

The sportsman class of racers don't get the same amount of air coming up over jumps as the Pro racers, so that they can keep in control of their sleds. It takes a lot of driver experience to be able to keep the sleds in position for a good landing, particularly if there is a wind. A headwind can lift the sled and flip it over backwards if the sled angle is too sharp, while side winds can contribute to a landing that throws a driver off the line he had planned.

The Duluth National snocross season opener attracts hundreds of drivers from across the United States and Canada. This photo shows the pit area, with a few classes getting ready for staging. There is no snow on the ground yet, so the course itself is created with the snow making machines from the Spirit Mountain ski resort. The ground, however, has some woodchips spread to make it easier on the carbides and studs of the machines.

This photo was taken in the Snowmobile Hall of Fame Museum. The 1993 sled was owned and driven by Curtis Friede of Seeley Lake, Montana. You can see it is a hill climbing sled, with the extremely long track—much of which is behind the driver's seat. Friede won numerous hill climbing awards including Jackson Hole World Champion; Washington State Champion; Canadian Champion; Missoula, Montana Champion; and the Fernie, British Columbia Championship.

These two semi-pro drivers are getting some good air as they come over the hill at the Duluth National snocross event. Jarett Kimball, the #292 driver on a Polaris, is from Genoa City, Wisconsin. He first started racing sleds in 2001, and trains by riding motocross bikes in the off-season. Thatcher Haggberg, on the #42 Arctic Cat, is from Nestor Falls, Ontario. With a summer job as a fishing guide, he spends a lot of time in the outdoors.

The starter has just dropped the flag and this Pro race is underway. The holeshot seems to be a three-way tie between an Artic Cat, Polaris, and a Ski-doo. Ryan Simons, on the #67, races out of Sedgewick, Alberta. Duluth, Minnesota, driver Matt Judnick is on the Polaris. He was one of only two Polaris drivers to finish in the top 10 Pro Open WSA class points race in 2003–2004. You can see the drivers all squeezing to a center line as they take the short sprint to the first tight turn.

Willie Elam, on board his #130 Ski-Doo rides with the Blair Morgan Racing team. With a hometown in Buhl, Idaho, he got a lot of track time in racing with RMXCRC, taking lots of high point awards through 2001 to 2004, including 2004 RMXCRC Pro High Points Champion.

The Winnipeg Canadian Open Snocross race provided for lots of bumping in this tight corner. The WPSA snocross series usually consists of about 10 races, with two of the race sites in Canada and the others in locations across the United States. Some of the longest running races include the Ski-Doo Grand Prix de Valcourt, Valcourt, Quebec; Amsoil Duluth National, Duluth, Minnesota; Canterbury Snocross, Shakopee, Minnesota; and the Nielsen Enterprises Grand Finale, Lake Geneva, Wisconsin.

Levi LaVallee won the 2004 Winter X Games HillCross championship on January 27, 2004 in Aspen, Colorado. It was only the second Hill-Cross competition ever for then 21-year-old La-Vallee. He finished about three seconds ahead of X Games Hillcross 2004 silver medalist and fellow Polaris racer, Justin Tate, while Polaris racer D.J. Eckstrom finished fourth, and TJ Gulla was sixth. Gulla took an X Games Gold in Hillcross in 2003. LaVallee suffered a knee injury the following season in the Duluth National that kept him grounded for a year before returning to snocross and hill climbs.

Arctic Cat driver, Billy Waldoch (#333) is a machine length ahead of Polaris driver, Kyle Murphy (#284) in this heat race of the Semi-Pro Open class at the Duluth National snocross race. The Semi-Pro Open has qualified racers driving snowmobiles with a maximum displacement of 600 cc. Each sled must pass the safety inspection prior to the race. Waldoch's early career earned him a reputation for fast laps and large crashes.

The first tight turn of a snocross race proves a few things: who got the holeshot when the flag dropped; which sled is best dialled in for the current running conditions; and who has the best setup. This race in West Yellowstone can be challenging to flatlanders, or drivers who don't live in the mountains, since modifications are required to make sleds run well at the higher elevations.

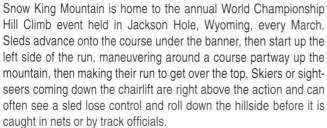

Snow King Mountain is home to the annual World Championship Hill Climb event held in Jackson Hole, Wyoming, every March. Sleds advance onto the course under the banner, then start up the left side of the run, maneuvering around a course partway up the mountain, then making their run to get over the top. Skiers or sightseers coming down the chairlift are right above the action and can often see a sled lose control and roll down the hillside before it is caught in nets or by track officials.

The staging area at the Jackson Hole Hill Climb is between the crowd and the hill. These sleds are lined up in front of the Jumbotron. Cameras feeding the Jumbotron are placed at strategic points on the hillside, so spectators can get an up-close view of some of the key moments of the race. Spectators usually use binoculars to gaze up the mountainside from their lawn chairs at the bottom of the hill, although a thousand or so take the ski lift to the top of the hill, then gradually walk down, watching from vantage points along the way.

This X Games photo shows teammates Blair Morgan and Carl Kuster in the air during the snocross event. Kuster was one of an early few select riders with hillcross, hill climb, and snocross skills. Morgan has been called the best and most influential rider in the history of the sport of snocross. Morgan claimed 74 of 140 Nat'l finals and 12 of 16 points titles between the 1997–1998 and 2004–2005 seasons. Photo credit to Jason Gilmour of *snoxmagazine.com*.

Iain Hayden rides the #93 Ski-Doo for the Royal Distributing/Factory Recreation snocross team. His home is in Espanola, Ontario. He was Pro Champion in 2003, in only his second year on the racetrack, and in 2005 for the CSRA snocross circuit in Canada. His summer pursuits include motocross, where he competes with the Suzuki team.

Tucker Hibbert, #68, soared to fame at the age of 15 when he won the X Games Gold in snocross. He continued to race snocross with the WSA for several years, becoming the 2001 Pro Open champ, 2002 Pro Open and Pro Stock champ, along with silver medals at the X Games in 2002, 2004, and 2005. While snocross continues to be just a sideline with Hibbert, he is fully committed to his supercross and motocross career. He lives in Centerville, Mississippi.

The riding style of all four of these semi-pro drivers is similar as they all get about equal amounts of air over the hill at the Duluth National snocross race. The flagman stands watch, waiting with his yellow flag in case of an accident or break-down. Once the yellow flag goes up passing is not allowed on the course through the area being flagged. Usually the track team will have the sled removed before drivers make another lap, but drivers must be on the look out to make sure the course isn't still under yellow. Passing under yellow means a disqualification for the race.

Kurtis Crapo, driver #9, first hit the racetrack in high school with an entry into a cross-country event. Racing out of St. Anthony, Idaho, he's had many wins in RMXCRC Snocross and Cross Country series races. Once Polaris' best snocross rider, Crapo struggled through injuries and sled problems for several years. His 2005 finish in the Top 10 in points in both Pro Open and Pro Stock on the WSA National circuit make him one of the drivers to beat with his Arctic Cat.

There's lots of action on the whoops here in this West Yellowstone RMXCRC event at the annual RMXCRC season final. Whoops is the term given to a series of moguls on a snocross track, and it's easy to see where it comes from if you take a look at the Arctic Cat driver about to go for a roll in the snow.

There's lots of snow flying as drivers compete for position in the last lap of this tight race. The Arctic Cat out front has his trigger pinned so his spinning track is throwing lots of wet snow, splattering into the face of the driver behind him. It was shirtsleeves weather on this last event of the year, so the snow had a very different texture than earlier in the season. Racers needed to change set-up to compensate for track conditions.

Earl Reimer, #100, is out front with his Ski-Doo in this race. Despite competing in the Pro Plus class for drivers over 35, Reimer's skills still kept him out front, qualifying and competing in WPSA Pro Classes as well as the X Games sno-cross events. The Pro sleds, as you can see from this photo, get a lot more air and land a lot further down the hill on this track at Duluth than the Semi-Pros who have less experience.

This photo of Carl Kuster, #47, was taken at Lake Geneva in 2005, which was his last snocross race with the Blair Morgan Racing Team. Kuster took the Gold Medal at the inaugural X Games Hillcross event in 2001, as well as Gold in 2002. He earned Silver in 2003 Hillcross and Bronz in the 2004 Hillcross event. Kuster also competed successfully in snocross with the WSA. Photo credit to Jason Gilmour of *snoxmagazine.com*

Steve Martin drives the #18 Ski-Doo. Martin is a great all-around rider who excels at snocross, hillcross, hill climb, and freeride. He earned two X Games medals in HillCross, the first captured at age seventeen in 2002. His 2004 season was cut short due to a back injury suffered in a horrific crash in the 2004 X Games snocross practice.

It seems in this photo like one line around this tight turn is preferable, as all of the sleds are lined up instead of being spread across the track. On this part of the course the driver throws his body off the sled to the inside of the turn, using his own weight to help him through the corner.

Blair Morgan captured the 2005 X Games Snocross Gold after finishing first in all of his heats. With his seventh consecutive medal in the very competitive event, Morgan set an all around X Games record, also becoming the second athlete to win four gold medals in the same X Games event. Morgan's accomplishment put him into the Guinness Book of World Records in 2005. Morgan broke his own record by winning the Gold again in 2006. Photo credit to Jason Gilmour of *snoxmagazine.com*.

These two snocross racers are both Semi-Pro drivers in a heat race. The WPSA uses a round robin qualifying and elimination format in all events. This means the drivers for each event are divided into heats, and race either two or three rounds. Finish positions are added together, with ties broken by counting the last round as the most and the first round as the least. Position in the final is determined from the heat races. If required, an LCQ or Last Chance Qualifier may be run, in order to fill the field.

D.J. Eckstrom, sled #25, has a reputation as an incredible model of consistency. Eckstrom only failed to make the top ten at the X Games just twice in 9 events (6 snocross, 3 hillcross). He earned nine podiums on the WSA National circuit in 2003–2004, second only to Blair Morgan. Between the 1999–2000 season and the end of the 2003–2004 season, he had 35 podiums, making him the third highest finisher in that span.

These two Semi-Pro drivers use different riding styles to take the hill here. Polaris driver #255, in the background, takes more air to land further down the hill, than the Polaris sled in the foreground. Racing for year-end points over the course of the season, they each want to finish as high as possible in their heat races, as well as making a podium finish if possible. When running the National Circuit all of a driver's points stay with a rider, while for the Manufacturer's Championship, the points stay with the sled.

D.J. Ekre, sled #52, is from Shevlin, Minnesota. His smooth driving style makes him a natural and a strong finisher in both cross-country racing and snocross. He rides with the Christian Brothers Racing team out of Fertile, along with teammate Matt Piche. The 2005–2006 WPSA snocross season marked his switch from Semi-Pro to Pro.

Notice the way the Arctic Cat rider out front throws his weight to the edge of the sled to help turn in this corner, using his handlebars to hang onto the sled as well as steer. WPSA rules allow drivers to use any commercially available handlebars even in the stock snocross classes. Handlebars may be altered to fit the driver, although open ends must be capped and the bars must be padded. Grips and controls may be modified, but snowmobiles are not allowed to use twist grips like motorcycles.

This snocross sled is under power, so only a very small portion of his track is on the snow. The track you see is studded for best traction on the hard surfaces. Rules restrict studs to being not more than 3/8 of an inch (1 cm) above the highest point of the track. No cleats or partial cleats may be added to tracks, and the length and width of the track must be as produced by the manufacturer.

Carl Schubitzke, #96, is one on the best snocross drivers riding for Polaris. Out of Duluth, Minnesota, Schubitzke is a member of the Amsoil/Red Bull/U.S. Air Force Scheuring Speed Sports team, along with D.J. Eckstrom. Schubitzke started driving Pro with WSA at fifteen, before the rules were changed to an age requirement of sixteen.

Steve Taylor, riding the #2 Ski-Doo with the Blair Morgan Racing Team, is from Prince George, British Columbia. The team's home base is Okotoks, Alberta, and is owned by Blair Morgan, Jamie Anseeuw, and Wayne Madsen. In this photo Steve is duelling it out with an Arctic Cat for position. Steve has struggled to stay healthy since sustaining a very serious concussion at the WSA Syracuse event in 2003.

Riders coming over the whoops part of the West Yellowstone snocross course spend a lot of time in the air. West Yellowstone's annual end-of-the-season race action runs along with the West Yellowstone Snowmobile Expo. The Expo is the big event of the year as snowmobile manufacturers take the opportunity to bring out the upcoming season's line-up for enthusiastic snowmobilers to preview. Other exhibitors cover every aspect of the snowmobile industry, from tourism to trail riding.

There's lots of action coming over the hill at this Duluth National race, as some drivers are still airborne, while others are starting to land. Notice the different styles as some drivers land close to flat, while others come down on the rear part of their tracks.

Matt Judnick, on the #58 Polaris, was one of just a few semi-pro racers to make the X Games 2002 field, which he qualified for by taking fifth at the WSA Duluth qualifier, his hometown race. The X Games Snocross event starts with a field of invited participants, based on the previous year's finishes, then holds qualifier events at the WSA National races to fill out the field.

This Ski-Doo driver didn't get a lot of air coming over the hill, but opted for a ride closer to the snow. Unlike riders who fly over this piece of the course, this driver is in a seated position instead of standing over the handlebars. This style of riding is closer to that used by cross-country racers.

Shaun Crapo, Arctic Cat sled #3, is the youngest of the three Crapo brothers with snocross racing experience—Jeremy and Kurtis are the other two. Shaun was Arctic Cat's choice to replace Tucker Hibbert, when Hibbert decided to leave snocross to focus on motocross. Shaun inherited Tucker's semi and ace crew, which has been very beneficial to his career.

Chapter 2
EXTREME ICE RACING

Modern ice oval racing is the F1 of the snow-mobile racing sport. Drivers, protected only with leather suits, pads, safety-jackets, and helmets, race just inches off the ice surface at speeds that often hit 100 miles per hour (162 kph). Relying on driver technique to control their sleds, as well as mechanical set-up, one wrong move can send a driver crashing into another sled or the hay-bale covered boards at extremely high speeds.

The Events

Extreme ice racing events use two different types of tracks: the lemans or oval. The ice lemans course layout is a boot shaped track 0.5 to 1 mile (0.8 km to 1.6 km) in length. Drivers line up from a starting point on the longest side and make a specified num-

ber of laps before finishing under a checkered flag. This type of track requires drivers to make both left and right hand turns.

Oval racetracks have varied by the venue over the years, but the current standard is a half-mile. An oval track is defined as a racecourse that includes two or four left hand turns on prepared, groomed, and maintained track. The difference arises from the length of the track on the ends of the ovals—if the distance is long there are two long sweeping turns at each corner, while a track with a very narrow end has one very sharp turn at each end.

Oval sprint racing is measured by laps, with a standard sprint race consisting of anywhere from three to fifteen for each class. Generally, elimination heats have fewer laps, as do junior and Women's

Jim Adams leads the pack through corner one at the Canadian Power Toboggan Championship race (CPTC) in Beausejour, Manitoba. Adams drives a Ski-Doo out of Rochester, Minnesota. With a racing career into its second decade, his worst crash was in the 2003 Valcourt Valentine's Day event, where he shattered both ankles and ended up in a wheelchair for four months.

classes. The twenty-five lap, or occasionally longer, race is usually a feature with the fastest class participating in the event. Sprint races may take place on a lake using natural ice, or on a track of prepared man-made ice.

Enduro races have more laps as designated by the venue. The Soo I-500 or International 500 Snowmobile Race features a 500-lap race, with each entrant machine timed. The sled may be driven by a team or a single driver may run the whole 500 laps. It takes the I-500 Racing group three weeks and 1,800,000 gallons of water to make the track. Water is transported from a hydrant in the pit area by three 8,000-gallon tankers and many trips sprinkling it around the track to create ice. After 29 years of manually counting the laps they now use an electronic system.

Four winning sleds from the Soo I-500 are on display in the Snowmobile Hall of Fame Museum. As time passes vintage oval racing gains more and more of an importance at sprint oval racing events. These machines are popular with drivers as they often provide a lower cost entry point for racing, or a way for veteran drivers to stay involved in a sport they have always loved. Vintage machines also allow spectators to compare the old with the new, and relive their own memories.

Driver Rules

Rules for drivers are established by individual governing bodies, affiliates, clubs or associations, with the ISR (International Snowmobile Racing) rules providing the standard. The WPSA and USSA have the largest extreme ice circuits. The rules begin with the age and qualifications of the individual driver including Amateur, Sportsman or Sport, Semi-Pro, Pro, and Masters (racers over a specified age). Women-only classes may be created in these skill level areas as well, although since there are fewer women involved in the sport there is often only an Amateur Women and Pro Women class, or Pro Women class alone.

Young competitors are encouraged in sprint oval racing with a full range of classes divided by age group: Junior 10–13; Junior I, ages 14–15; and Junior II, ages 16–17. The 120s, or child-sized sleds, may run on a smaller size oval track.

All drivers are required to wear safety equipment on the racetrack. The most important is a snell-approved full-face helmet, colored blaze orange, which

Jeff Mitchell, #330, is in the lead of these three Polaris sleds as they race around the oval track in the Semi-Pro Sprint Class. The USSA Sprint Class restricts engines to 500 cc or less in displacement. Engines can be taken from any 1978 or newer sled from Arctic Cat, Ski-Doo, Polaris, or Yamaha.

Todd Chartier, #39, heads to the checkered flag in the Sport 500 class with his Arctic Cat sled. Chartier is out of Fair Haven, Michigan. The Sport or Sportsman class provides a professional entry level for drivers.

Dale Planck drove his Ski-Doo, which he nicknamed "The Puffer," to first place in the inaugural International 500 or SOO I-500 in Sault Ste. Marie, Michigan, on February 8, 1969. His time was 13 hours, 42 minutes. The Puffer has a 669 cc Rotax engine under the hood. This sled is on display in the Snowmobile Hall of Fame Museum.

must be securely fastened and worn even in the tune-up area. Drivers in the Pro and Masters classes must have Blaze orange cover a specified portion of the driver's back and front, along with upper body protection. Motocross vests or hockey equipment do not meet the rule standards. Other mandatory items include: gloves, appropriate clothing, at least above ankle leather boots, shin and knee guards that cover from the instep to above the knee, and elbow pads are highly recommended. Eye protection is mandatory. Once dressed, the final thing the driver must wear is a racing bib or other form of garment marked with their issued number.

Snowmobile Rules

Sprint and Enduro oval rules for the safety features of snowmobiles are the same as those outlined in the Extreme Snow racing events.

The Evolution of Ice Oval Racing

Oval racing began as a way to test the handling of the snowmobile in turns and corners. Unlike cross-country racing, it also allowed spectators to watch the whole race, so rapidly became popular with promoters who wanted to sell everything from hot chocolate and hamburgers, to their own snowmobiles. Indeed, many of the first oval races culminated by giving spectators a turn to drive around the infield with one of the new-fangled toys for grown-ups and kids alike.

Mike Bosak, of Brokenhead, Manitoba, built and sold twenty to thirty Bosak Motor Toboggans each year, from 1950 through the early 1960s. Nearby Beausejour, which always had a winter festival each February, decided to include a power toboggan race on its 1962 agenda. An oval course was laid out with bales in the snow-covered schoolyard, with six drivers competing at speeds up to 15 miles per hour (24 kph). The event was a hit, and organizers formally registered its title as the Canadian Power Toboggan Championships [CPTC] in 1963. CPTC, still held annually, is the oldest race in the sport's history.

Like Beausejour's, the early tracks were all snow surfaces, with later ones generally banked to help the drivers turn. Steering in the first snowmobiles had a long way to go to meet modern standards, plus traction products were non-existent. Spectators stood eagerly on the sidelines, held off the track by snow bales or sheets of plyboard.

In 1966 the Eagle River Lions Club built the first-ever snowmobile oval racetrack on Highway 45 on the outskirts of Eagle River, Wisconsin. The property, leased from Pleasure Island, had been rodeo grounds some years earlier. It required only slight modifications to be hailed as the best oval racing environment in the world. Indeed, some called the derby the Indianapolis of snowmobile racing. The first Eagle River World's Championship title went to Steve Ave on a Ski-Doo.

But everyone wanted to hold a "world series" race. The Canadian Player's cigarette company made large contributions through the 1966-1967 racing season, offering open class winners expenses-paid trips to the Player's World in Montreal, Quebec, in March of 1967. Participants competed in three events for a total points victory: closed-course cross-country, slalom, and 20-lap oval. Steve Ave once again took the title on a Ski-Doo.

Shane Peterson, riding Polaris sled #99, leads the field of six Semi-Pro Formula drivers through this corner. It was all Shane Peterson as he earned first place spots in both the Semi Pro Champ 440 class and the Semi Pro Formula 600 class in the 2005–2006 season opener in Beausejour, Manitoba. Riding a 2005 Wahl built sled, the Lancaster, Minnesota, resident pushed past his competition to victory.

With so much enthusiasm for the sport, the fledgling United States Snowmobile Association (USSA) had everything in place to sanction race events and provide leadership for the rapidly expanding world of racing by December of 1967. Crandon, Wisconsin, had the honor of being the first race of the season. But, things didn't go as planned, since the tech man they'd lined up failed to appear—a local Jeep dealer from Eagle River, Bud Powell, pitched in and went home for his tools to help. The race, held on the lake, seemed doomed right from its rocky start. By Sunday it was raining and the lake looked treacherous to the USSA officials. They sent Steve Ave out to make practice laps at his fastest speed and report on the conditions. He declared the track unsafe, so John Hull, Race Director, called the event. Amidst the furor from angry drivers, racetrack safety became an integral part of the USSA's racing mandate.

A new craze soon grew up in oval racing—the Enduro. The (Soo) I-500, held in Sault Ste. Marie,

Michigan, is the longest running race of this type. It debuted on February 8, 1969, the day the fares on the Mackinaw Bridge went from $3.50 to $1.50. The race was packed with spectators, most sure the machines would never make 200 miles, let alone 500. Organizers established their own rules, based on those from the Indianapolis 500 car race. After 13 hours and 42 minutes, Ski-Doo driver, Dan Planck of Davidson completed the 500th lap. By the time he finished, only 26 machines were still running, having completed a total of 13,891 miles (22,226 km) showing that snowmobiles truly were in for the long haul.

In terms of long, the Montpelier, Quebec 24-hour Endurance Race held in 1969 was one of the longest—at least time-wise. The winners, Leonide Jodoin, Clement Morier, and Yvon Jodoin, piloted a stock Scorpion Sting around 710 laps to emerge as winners. Traverse City and Alpena, Michigan, both held 250-mile Enduros in 1970. Polaris sleds won

Notice the driver in this photo is wearing all of the standard safety gear required to go on the track in an extreme ice oval event. The Blaze orange color has been required for decades since it is the easiest color to see in ice fog. Drivers, like this one, who crash in an event are also easy to identify on the track, so oncoming drivers can swerve to avoid them.

both events, ridden by Denny Nelson and Rolane Hanes, establishing Polaris at the forefront for that winter season.

Eager oval racers weren't to be limited by the seasons, however, and even tried summer racing on a woodchip track—where else, of course, but Wisconsin? The USSA sanctioned a one-third mile woodchip oval event at Three Lakes on July 1 and 2, 1972. Ed Schubitzke drove his Ski-Doo to win the Oval Worlds' Summer Championship title. Later, Eagle River promoters repeated the summer event with the 1986 Wood Chip Classic.

Promoters were anxious to get involved, and winter racers soon picked their choice of sprint tracks and locations: either flat track ice surfaces on lakes, or banked hard packed snow surfaces on specially built or existing race facilities. But a heat wave before the 1973 Eagle River Derby accidentally brought about a refinement in track surfaces. Watching the snow melt organizers grew frantic—the race by now had a

A snowmobile set up to race on the ice oval is very different from either a trail machine or a snocross sled. Oval racing sleds are very close to the ice, since they don't require the same kind of suspension as drivers flying or bouncing over bumps. Oval sleds also have very short skis, as you can see here. Sleds are decaled with sponsors' trademarks and names.

This is the underside of an oval sled's track. You can see the numerous studs that have been installed for traction on the ice. You will also note that the pattern isn't even—instead studs are distributed in a way that makes the sled better handling through the corners. Some of the very earliest traction products used included such things as screws through the track.

In an oval race all of the sleds enter the track from the pits and travel to the start line, where they line up in the lanes they have drawn—lane 1 is the inside lane that borders the infield. Jacques Villeneuve #96, has that position in this line-up. The Race Director must get a ready nod from each driver, so he glances to each one in turn, moving to the next at the nod. Once all of the drivers are ready he either drops the flag or brings it up off the ice, whichever style he uses.

reputation to maintain, and the community relied on the tourism it generated with 25,000 and more spectators. They decided to try covering the track with sawdust to sop up the water and protect the snow as much as possible. When the weekend arrived the temperature dropped and the mixture froze into a hard surface. Not only was it good for speed, but it also reduced the amount of snowdust that formed through a race. The new surface soon became a standard for oval racers.

Indeed, 1973 marked a turning point that focused the snowmobile racing world's attention on the oval racetrack. It took a combination of variables, including the high speeds stock machines could now reach with their "big honker" engines, making races more and more dangerous; a backlog of manufactured unsold machines at the end of a warm winter; and ultimately, the world's first fuel shortage.

The USSA invited manufacturers to sit at the table and discuss their options. Fourteen were voting

This photo illustrates the style used by drivers to corner at high speeds. You can see that the driver swings his body as far as possible to the left side of the sled as he makes the sharp left hand turn into the corner. This helps the machine corner, plus helps hold the snowmobiles track on the ice.

Spectators still stand trackside at an ice oval event, however there are mandatory safety barriers between the sleds and the crowd. Hay bales are the first line, often in a double row at the corners, since hay minimizes the impact of a crash both on the sled and the driver. Chain link fence keeps the crowd a safe distance away from this field of vintage sleds.

members of the organization including: Mercury, Arctic Cat, Ski-Doo, Polaris, Speedway, Columbia, Alouette, Yamaha, Alsport, SnoJet, Kohler, and Leisure Vehicles. One of the end results was the creation of a SnoPro racing class that would have professional drivers and specially produced racing sleds, paving the way for manufacturers to stop putting ever more powerful engines in the stock machines. The USSA also created a stock quantity rule that limited the eligibility of manufacturer's models to race certain classes. SnoJet took the USSA and the big three, Polaris, Bombardier, and Arctic Cat to court over the rule. The judge's decision validated the growth of snowmobile racing from what he called sandlot to major league, and maintained the ruling. SnoPro was born.

The first SnoPro race was held on December 9, 1973, at Ironwood, Michigan. In addition to the factories, there were twenty independent racers building all kinds of modified sleds for the new class. The machine that was to have the most lasting effect on the world of racing was Gilles Villeneuve's Alouette twin tracker with its independent front suspension—and its unique looks were certainly a crowd pleaser. Stan Hayes took the 340 class on a Polaris, Lynn Trapp on his Yamaha won the 440, and Bob Eastman the 650 race.

But it didn't take long until they discovered SnoPro represented an extremely high cost to drivers and the factories. The original SnoPro circuit design was replaced by the Professional Drivers Circuit in 1975—the name SnoPro however, continued to be used for many seasons to come. The change simply meant that drivers planning to attend all of the big events bought a $100 professional membership that kept them from competing in the smaller, non-sanctioned events. Drivers could still compete wherever they wanted simply by paying the appropriate lower amateur fee of $25—but then they weren't eligible for the point fund created out of the additional money. The SnoPro classes to run were Supermod and 440X.

By 1976 SnoPro racing was in full swing. Tuning began in Alaska as soon as the temperature fell and the snow flew. Testing meant lots of changes that year to add independent front suspensions, which nay-sayers insisted would never be a mass-produced thing for trail machines, but had to admit seemed essential on the racetrack. With improved handling racing got even better.

The 1977–1978 racing season was an interesting one, with drivers changing brands, and manufacturers thinking of new ways to get the most for their buck in promotion. Mercury Sno-Twisters had been the surprise winners on the previous year's tracks, but it wasn't enough to keep a flailing company from sinking, and it went out of business. Ski-Doo, which had been watching instead of playing for the previous two years, signed on the Merc drivers: Doug and Stan Hayes, along with Ed Schubitzke, who'd won the 1977 World Championship as an independent on a Yamaha. Leroy Linblad rounded out the factory team they hoped would take a quick trip to the top. Yamaha were funding Dick Trickle and Bobby Donahue. Brad Hulings (shifted from Merc), Jim Bernat, Jerry Bunke, and Don Ohmdahl were on a Polaris sponsored team.

But nobody counted on a scarlet fever—Scorpion invasion, sweeping SnoPro racing in the 1978–1979 season. Both the Polaris and Yamaha factories had left the playground with their support budgets that year, so Scorpion had been a welcome addition. Between Brad Hulings and teammate, Steve Thorsen, they dominated the early season, with Hulings matching his 1976–1977 season record of six consecutive victories—only he'd been riding a Polaris on the Midnight Blue Express that conquered SnoPro two years earlier. But the red turned color when the Black Magic racing team took over, with Bob Elsner leading the way on his Arctic Cat on the SnoPro circuit.

The 1979 SnoPro circuit tour ended with expenses-paid trips from the Swedish snowmobile distributors Aktiv, Movac and Yamaha, plus Sno-Skoter magazine, for the top drivers for two weeks to Scandinavia. The first ice oval sprint race was in Rovaniemi, Finland, on March 1, with the second in Umea, Sweden, for a mid-week program, and the final one on March 8 in Ostersund, Sweden. Hulings swept the entire Scandinavian series, with teammate Thorsen in second, and Dimmerman in third on his Arctic Cat, taking the wins over the Scandinavian drivers. SnoPro racing was truly global.

Across the wide spectrum of racing the issue of rules continued, which resulted in the formation of the WSRF or World Snowmobile Racing Federation, in 1979. The six existing North American manufacturers paid cash dues totalling $64,000 as a start-up fund, with another $12,000 to be used exclusively on safety research in racing. The main portion of the money was used to start an office and hire an ad-

The earliest models of snowmobiles often had trouble making a whole race without breaking down, so it wasn't uncommon to have a leading machine stop, change a belt, then jump back into the race to still place in the top finalists. This vintage racer is repeating history in more ways than one!

ministrator to coordinate and supervise oval track sprint and endurance racing, along with cross-country in North America and abroad. Bill Vint was the first Executive Director. Dick Gokey was president of the WSRF Board of directors, with Vice Presents Andy van Dolder (Ontario), Dick Decker (Wisconsin), and Harvey Waldron III (Washington). Walter Gretschman of Manitoba was secretary; Bob Chisholm (Massachusetts) treasurer, and Assistant Treasurer, Bill Hyland (Wisconsin). The federation had most of the major regional divisions join, including the USSA (largest racing group in North America at that time), and others from all over Canada and the United States. The largest group to reject the WSRF was the International Cross-Country Snowmobile Federation or ICSF.

The first year of racing with the WSRF rules-making body was the 1980–1981 season. Although they adopted most of the USSA rules, there were some no-

This driver makes a checkered flag victory lap around the Eagle River Derby Track—home of the World Championship, which expanded its January event to include a seventeen day celebration of racing that includes a whole vintage weekend. Pro Vintage Racing Inc., dedicated to keeping pro vintage racing sleds on the track, has been around for sixteen years keeping the competition as keen as it ever was. Two hundred and fifty members strong, Pro Vintage classes include everything built from the 1960s right through to 1985. Their key event is the Eagle River Championship.

table changes. This year marked the introduction of the special performance rating charts that put sleds into different classes for drag racing and oval racing, depending on their handling characteristics. Some would say this wasn't fair—while others were generally pleased with the ratings. SnoPro saw the elimination of the 250 and 440X classes, which were replaced with two limited horsepower classes, the 340 cc (55 hp) and 440 cc (70 hp) Formula oval classes.

Twin track snowmobiles dominated the fastest oval racing of the 1980s, both in sprint and enduro. A Ski-Doo twin-track sled won the Soo I-500 in 1981, with close competition from a Yamaha. Scorpion's twin-tracker took the WSRF SnoPro series championship that year. Seven of the top sleds in the SnoPro class had been twin-trackers, with Jim Dimmerman still on an Arctic Cat single track in second place. The new designs from Ski-Doo and Moto-Ski for 1982 featured twin track machines with the driver over one of the tracks, so he could maneuver his body as though driving a single track sled. The twin track era was coming to life.

The WSRF was doomed to a short life, and died shortly, along with factory sponsorship of SnoPro racing. The ISR or International Snowmobile Racing, Inc. was formed in 1981 to coordinate services for the independent snowmobile race groups and

This vintage racer proudly wears all of his original gear while driving his MOD V Polaris sled. The four-digit number on his racing bib is testament to the number of registered racers during the haydays of snowmobile racing. His helmet is a full face, like modern requirements, but the face shield is several generations behind modern styles. Beneath his visor you would see several overlapping layers of duct tape over his nose, to vent his breath out the bottom of the helmet in order to keep it from fogging during the race.

The race leader in this vintage class is #54x, driven by Dick Peterson of Elk River, Minnesota. Peterson is one of the drivers to beat in the leaf spring free-air classes with his 1973 Polaris. The sled immediately behind Peterson is a Rupp. Rupp, an American company operating out of Mansfield, Ohio, was the dreamchild of Mickey Rupp. From their first year in 1959 to their last year in 1978, the Rupp company produced snowmobiles, minibikes, ATVs, and three wheeled motorized tricycles with a high amount of both quality and style.

This photo was taken in the Snowmobile Hall of Fame Museum. The sled is #699, a Ski-Doo owned and raced by Loren Anderson. Anderson began racing in 1967, running Rupp sleds, before switching to Ski-Doo Blizzards in the 1971-1972 season. When he stopped racing himself he became the Team Manager for his son, Bob Anderson. The original truck and trailer Bob used, fully stocked including the twin-tracker sled, is part of the Snowmobile Hall of Fame Museum in St. Germain, Wisconsin.

manufacturers, the majority of whom joined the ISR as voting members. The ISR office is in West Bend, Wisconsin, and is still fulfilling its mandate. During the more than two and a half decades since its inception three men have been at the forefront of the ISR: Dick Gokey, Tom Zernia, and Olav Aaen. The focus over the years has been on helping clubs and organizations run snowmobile races in an organized and safe manner.

Snowmobile clubs were struggling with those same issues across the country. In Eagle River the Lions Club, who'd run the World Championship since

its inception, were faced with more work than the volunteer association could handle. The racetrack was sold to the Decker racing family in 1985, who continued to expand the racing events and manage the World Championship race each winter.

For the winter of 1987-1988, the big news was the birth of the Ski-Doo NGK Sport Series, which shot new energy into the independents on the Sno-Pro twin-track sleds, who had been running regionally, instead of at a National level. The series had $35,000 in point fund money to be spread over ten races in Canada and the United States. Some of the most colourful racing ever to hit the circuit appeared, as twin-track sleds in pinks, blues, and every other shade that would stand out on the racetrack, zipped around the ice hitting over 100 mph (160 kph). A new generation—and some from the old—made the headlines in the Sport Series: Jacques Villeneuve, Jim Appolson, along with many family teams, the Deckers, the Goodwins, the Vessairs, the van Dolders, and the Wahls. It was like oval racing had a new breath of life.

In the 1990-1991 oval racing season, four sprint racers were included in the top ten list of drivers by *Snow Week*. Mike Houle, the 1989-1990 *Snow Week* Driver of the year once again made the list, for capturing both Chevy Pro Star class championships: F-III, and Pro Sprint. Often called one of the sport's true gentlemen, Gary Vessair was named after capturing the Ski-Doo Formula I Sport Series title. Setting aside the mods for the stock racing classes, Lanny Benoit chalked up 39 wins over the season, to earn himself a place in history. Jim Herzig earned the USSA circuit's Number One bib for a strong season on that competitive circuit to round out the list.

Competition remained keen over the next years, with the 26th running of the annual World Series of Oval Racing in Coniston, Ontario, March 2 and 3, 1996 being just one of many successful races. Coniston took the event after the first host was unable to carry through. Running later than originally intended, various scheduling conflicts made the turn-out of drivers lower than usual—but there was still plenty of speed and action to carry the weekend. The Formula I class, still running after a decade and a half, went to Dave Wahl after his nephew, Terry Wahl, blew a drive belt two laps from the finish. Second went to Dale Loritz, third to Darcy Ewing, and fourth to Mike Weatherill. Formula III was an easy victory for

The SnoJet Thunder Jet is one of the most well known of the early racing sleds. Shortly after Conroy Company purchased SnoJet snowmobiles, an engineer named Duane Aho was given a special job. He was responsible for the conception, design, and development of the new racing snowmobile model. The sled featured an aircraft aluminum tunnel, and was very low and wide. It provided testing grounds for the stock machines, trying out the new technologies like disc brakes and lightweight aluminum.

Mike Houle, followed by Brian Sturgeon, Wayne Nicholson, and Jim Herzig in fourth. The Champ 440, a growing class, went to Jim Schmidt, with Mike Houle in second, and Jeff Ludwig in third. A new season of drivers had emerged.

One thing drivers knew was that sometimes the unexpected happens—even on the ice oval. On January 21, 2001 fame came to two Saskatchewan drivers: Jeremy Johnston from Arcola, and Chris Hortness from Beinfait, when they placed first and second in the Eagle River World Championship. It was the first one-two finish by teammates at Eagle River since Al Fenhaus and Greg Goodwin had done it in 1993. Both Johnston and Hortness used a Wahl Chassis for their sleds with a Ski-Doo engine under the hood. The third place finisher, Jason Looker, admitted his goal had been to make the final, but surprised himself by ending up on the podium. Johnson's victory on the racetrack hadn't been without challenges though, since he'd spent a couple of years on the sidelines after a snocross accident nearly cost him a leg, and then a crash had taken him out of the 2000 World Championship race.

Indeed, the tough moments can make or break a racer's career, and for Russ Chartrand, who'd run the SOO I-500 twenty-three times already, with his best place a thirteenth finish in 1992, it seemed there were a lot more tough ones than good ones. One of the crowd favorites, Chartrand hoped for the best when he entered the 2001 event. After logging over 3,000 miles (4800 km) on the track, he certainly knew his way around! With a sixth place start, he and teammate Tim Leeck (on his tenth shot at the SOO) drove their Polaris 600 to victory in 8 hours, 14 minutes, and 35 seconds. It was a victory that certainly inspired racers in for the long haul.

As 2005 rolled around, oval racing had lots of excitement. P.J. Wanderscheid (World Champion in 2002, 2003, and 2006), took the Champ 440 high points title for the USSA racing association. Terry Wahl took the same title for the WSA Xtreme Ice Racing circuit.

In Enduro ice oval racing the 2005 Midwest International Racing Association (MIRA) top honors went to Jeff Longton for the 700 Mod Class and the 440 Champ. Dan Avery took three titles: Sportsman

Polaris sleds dominate this vintage class in Beausejour, Manitoba. There are various classes of vintage machines. The Relic Class is restricted to machines that are 1970 and older. Early Model Classes are for sleds to 1975 or older. Vintage Mod classes are restricted to 1979 and older and only machines with leaf spring design. Pro Vintage IFS classes are for machines built between 1977 and 1982, and may have independent front suspension. Late Models are sleds 1983 and older, having leaf spring front suspension, air cooled, stock production models with a 600 cc maximum.

Enduro, Sportsman Stock 600 Sprint and Sportsman Stock 500 Sprint. The points championship for the MIRA Mod 600 Enduro class was a year-long battle, with the victory decided at the last race of the season. Jeff Leuenberger of the Cadarette Racing team earned this Enduro title.

The 37th running of the SOO I-500 Enduro ran under spring-like conditions that were totally unexpected on the Sault Ste. Marie, Michigan track in 2005. Even with a lean field of just 31 sleds, the track soon deteriorated into one of the roughest in the SOO history as carbides and studs took their toll along with the weather. Yellow flag after yellow flag slowed the elapsed race time along with the less-than-great running conditions. By lap 113 race officials had to red flag the race to fix the transponders on two sleds that were supposed to be counting laps. The race took 8 hours, 43 minutes, and 7 seconds to complete.

At the completion of the final lap, four-time Soo champ Corey Davidson drove the No. 16 Polaris sled, owned by Gabe Bunke, across the finish line to claim over $12,000 in winnings. He repeated the victory in 2006, riding a new Yamaha sled. Josh Davis was the team's backup driver. More than $37,000 was awarded in prizes, making the year a good one for all of the winners.

As the 2005–2006 season began there was big news and big upcoming prizes for oval sprint racers. The "2006 Millenium Technologies and Vforce Reed Valve Systems Oval Challenge," a four-race series with $25,000 added, had been lined up. Todd Achterberg worked with oval circuits across the country to set up the slate at some of the biggest races of the season: Beausejour, Manitoba; Plymouth and Eagle River, Wisconsin; and Valcourt, Quebec.

Indeed, oval racing, while not as big as it once was, still had lots of dedicated racers out after some of the longest-running championships in the world of the sport.

This 433 Yamaha is in the Snowmobile Hall of Fame Museum. It was owned and raced by Mike Trapp. Completely restored, this is the sled that won the 1971 World Championship race at Eagle River. The feature, dubbed the most exciting race in history, was 15 laps long, with 13 lead changes. 1971 was the first year a timed lap on the oval track was used in qualifying to reduce the field from the 48 semi-finalists to the nine, plus the previous year's winner, who would run the final. It was also the first year that a standing start was used for the big race, instead of the flying start of previous events. The duel of the day was between Mike Trapp, with his smaller Yamaha, and Yvon DuHamel, riding a 795 cc Rotax Ski-Doo for the factory. This race is still remembered and talked about!

Bruce Rosentrader, #96, of Beausejour, Manitoba rides this 1973 Polaris. These Polaris sleds have been winning since they were first manufactured, as they were used in cross-country, oval, and drag racing events. Owner's manuals at the time warned drivers that if they opened up the sled, to hang on. As well as production Polaris models of this era, there are also rare limited-build, proto-type, and experimental sleds that have been collected by vintage enthusiasts looking for Polaris muscle sleds.

This start line crash action that took out a SnoJet and a Ski-Doo was the first heat race, of the first day of racing at the Loadmaster Classic Vintage Weekend on the Eagle River Derby Track in 2003. While many of the sleds racing may have been long-forgotten, their run to glory is far from over. Brands out on the ice in Eagle River that weekend included Scorpions, Rupps, Alouettes, Vikings, Skiroules, Mercury, Moto-Ski, John Deere, Manta, and all four of today's manufacturers.

Memorable Moments in Oval Racing

Steve Ave's 370 cc Ski-Doo was sponsored by a local garage for the first running of the World Championship in Eagle River in January of 1966. He'd already been racing since 1961, so wasn't intimidated by the big contingent of Ski-Doo executives with their fancy yellow suits and chartered airplanes full of people that arrived for the race. But it was Ave that Ski-Doo chose to drive their secret new machine. Ave, however, didn't agree to take the machine until an after-dark test run against his own snowmobile.

The new Ski-Doo snowmobile performed well for Ave and he qualified easily for the five-man field that would race ten laps to determine the first World's Champion. Excited about the $15,000 in prize money, Ave prepared for the start line. With everyone else waiting on the track, the Ski-Doo's recoil rope broke. The two-minute warning clock started counting down. Kaupi, a friend of Ave, quickly pulled the rawhide lace out of his boots and wrapped it around the starter. One tug broke the lace, but the snowmobile was running.

In the early laps it looked like Ave still wasn't going to get the victory. Then Ave noticed that the snow was hard packed on the banks where the thousands of people in the crowd were watching, right on the edge of the track. Creeping higher and higher up the embankment, Ave raced nearly on the boot laces of

the spectators. In the end he beat Randy Hites on his Polaris, by a foot. Steve Ave became the first World Champion of snowmobile racing.

The 1974 Eagle River World Championship Derby featured a new half-mile oval track to go along with the new SnoPro class. Gilles Villeneuve had a game plan ready for his Alouettes: they were drilled out and stripped down to the bare minimum to make them as light as possible. He intended to run the twin-tracker in the Modified class, then switch things back to run the 650cc three-cylinder for the Sunday afternoon World Championship race.

Gilles took the twin-tracker out for two SnoPro heats, then set about making modifications to the other sleds in his fleet, since the independent front suspension twin-track sled kept derailing on the tight corners. The new technology he'd been working on included open chain cases, with gears held in place by quick-release pins, and he'd put it on all his sleds. Although he hadn't taken much in the big SnoPro classes of the weekend, he'd made it through the eliminations with his three-cylinder 650cc racer for his chance at the world championship.

The field Villeneuve faced was strong, including three Polaris drivers, four Arctic Cat, and two Yamahas. Bright yellow Ski-Doos were noticeably absent, having withdrawn for the year due to the fuel crisis. And then, there was the one lone Alouette in the rapidly shrinking field of highly competitive snowmobile manufacturers. Gilles Villeneuve was the lone Canadian, representing the lone Canadian snowmobile manufacturer at the race. He was ready to win.

All ten drivers faced the race director on the starting line, nine decked in the newest innovation—racing leathers. The factory SnoPro teams were about looking like you were the top dog on the block, after all, so each driver wore color co-ordinated and styled leather snowmobile suits, consisting of jackets and bib-front pants, to match their sleds. Leather, racers had already discovered, gave them the best movement and comfort of any material. Villeneuve, wearing bib number 3469, with its Quebec flag emblazoned in the top lefthand corner, was on the other hand, an independent with an almost non-existent budget, but he was determined.

The start was what the spectators expected, and a disappointment for Villeneuve, as Coltom led through the first corner. Indeed, Villeneuve's twin tracker was only running on two cylinders! Once the third one kicked in, the race rapidly changed, with Villeneuve leaping to the front of the pack. Nobody could catch him. The crowd cheered, although they didn't know the name of the driver on the bright red sled. Even the announcer on the PA system couldn't quite figure out who was leading the race. But by the time the 1974 world-championship race ended, the name of Villeneuve had made an impact on snowmobile racing that rippled through the coming decades.

Another memorable moment in oval racing took place in 1995 when Terry Wahl of Greenbush, Minnesota, won the largest purse in snowmobile racing history. Winning 3 of 4 select races on the Boswell Super Sled Series, he took home a bonus check for $50,000.00 at the year-end banquet in Minneapolis, Minnesota. This was in addition to his earnings during the season races. It was a black-tie event. The Super Sled Series was the brain child of former racer and airline pilot for Northwest, J. Scott Mondus of Lakeville, Minnesota. Bringing oval racing to television at a professional level, Mondus had employed the marketing skills of Loren Anderson to line up one of the largest series sponsorships in history. The television shows set a new standard for snowmobile racing coverage. With onboard cameras, driver interviews, tech sections, race trailer visits and professional autograph sessions, the fans loved the Super Sled Series and it became a must see on ESPN television.

Who's in the Hall of Fame from Oval Racing?

The sport of snowmobile racing has had more impact on the growth of the snowmobile industry than any other one factor. Not only is the evolution of the machine itself due to refinements made for racing, but the safety equipment and clothing also changed as a direct result of snowmobile racing. Even the economic survival of today's four snowmobile brands can be traced to their success at competitions. It is no wonder then, that snowmobile race drivers have a special place in the annuls of snowmobile history.

Adema, Jim -- An original inductee in 1988. Raced SnoJet.

Ave, Steve – An original inductee in 1988. Raced Ski-Doo.

Bender, Tim – Inducted in 1999. Rode Yamaha and Polaris.

Bernat, Jim – Inducted in 1991. Rode Polaris.

Bloom, Gene – Inducted in 2004. Rode Rupp.

Bunke, Jerry – Inducted in 1996. Rode Polaris.

Coltom, Larry – Inducted in 1995. Rode Arctic Cat.

Cormican, Dale – Inducted 1997. Rode Arctic Cat Panthers, John Deere, Polaris, and Ski-Doo.

Desrosiers, Claude – Inducted in 2000. Rode Ski-Doo.

Donahue, Bobby – Inducted in 1997. Drove Yamaha, Kawasaki, and Ski-Doo.

DuHamel, Yvon – An original inductee in 1988. Rode Ski-Doo.

Earhart, Tom – Inducted in 1994. Raced Rupp, Speedway, Polaris, and Arctic Cat.

Eastman, Bob – An original inductee in 1988. Rode Polaris.

Eck, Duane – Inducted in 1990. Rode Ski-Doo, Arctic Cat, and Polaris.

Elsner, Bob -- An original inductee in 1988. Rode Arctic Cat.

Ewing, Darcy – Inducted 2006. Raced Arctic Cat, Ski-Doo Kawasaki.

Frandsen, Duane – Inducted in 1992. Rode Ski-Doo.

Hayes, Doug – Inducted in 1996. Rode Polaris, Mercury, and Ski-Doo.

Hayes, Stan – An original inductee in 1988. Rode Ski-Doo, Mercury and John Deere.

Hulings, Brad – inducted in 1999. Rode Mercury, Polaris, Scorpion, and Ski-Doo.

This SnoPro sled is part of the collection in the Snowmobile Hall of Fame Museum. It was driven by both Stan Hayes and Doug Hayes from 1976 on. Hand-built in 1975, this 340 SnoPro Racer is one of only eight of its kind. The engine is a Kohler 340, while the chassis is an all aluminium lightweight design. It has a low profile hood and unique front suspension design.

This photo was taken at CPTC in Beausejour, Manitoba. The lead sled is a 3D Rupp, and is followed by a Mercury Sno-Twister and an Arctic Cat that seems to be running a modern hood on its vintage chassis.

Janssen, Roger – An original inductee in 1988. Raced Arctic Cat, Chaparral, John Deere, and Polaris.

Karpik, Gerard – Inducted in 1994. Rode Mercury and Ski-Doo.

Kirts, Dan – Inducted in 1995. Rode Manta.

Linblad, Leroy – Inducted in 1992. Rode Polaris and Ski-Doo.

Lofton, Charlie – Inducted in 1991. Raced Arctic Cat.

Mercer, Dorothy – Inducted in 1993. Raced Polaris.

Muetz, Gordy – Inducted in 2001. Rode Yamaha.

Musselman, Brian – Inducted in 1998. Rode Polaris, Ski-Doo, and Arctic-Cat.

Nelson, Brian – Inducted in 2000. Rode Polaris, Ski-Doo, Arctic Cat, and John Deere.

Rosenquist, Frans - Inducted 2006. Raced Ski-Doo, Sno-Jet, Mercury, Yamaha, Polaris, Kawasaki, Arctic Cat.

Rugland, Larry – Inducted in 1990. Rode Polaris and Ski-Doo.

Schubitzke, Ed – Inducted in 1993. Rode Ski-Doo, Polaris, Yamaha, and Mercury.

Dave Thompson – An original inductee in 1988. Drove Arctic Cat.

Mike Trapp – An original inductee in 1988. Raced Scorpion, Yamaha, and Ski-Doo.

Useldinger, Guy – Inducted in 2001. Rose Arctic Cat, Polaris, Yamaha, and Ski-Doo.

Villeneuve, Gilles – An original inductee in 1988. Raced Moto-Ski, Alouette, Skiroule.

Wahl, Dave – Inducted in 2005. Rode Arctic Cat, John Deere, Ski-Doo, and Polaris.

Wahl, Durmont – Inducted in 2005. Rode Arctic Cat, Ski-Doo, and Polaris.

Wicht, John – Inducted in 2003. Rode Kawasaki and Polaris.

Yancey, Herb – Inducted in 2002. Rode Husky, Ski-Doo, Arctic Cat, Polaris.

OVAL RACING'S AMAZING FACTS:

• The March, 1969, Canadian Power Toboggan Championships in Beausejour, Manitoba were filmed for a half hour feature by the Wide World of Sports.

• Dan Planck and his team won the first Soo I-500 in 1969 with an average speed of 36 mph, in a time of 13 hours, 42 minutes, and 12 seconds. He drove a 1969 Ski-Doo TNT.

• The permanent track racing surface at the Canadian Power Toboggan Championships in Beausejour, Manitoba, was switched to solid ice instead of packed snow for its 1976 race.

• The 1977 Eagle River World Champion, Steve Thorsen of Fergus Falls, Minnesota, set a new track record, averaging 85 mph (136 kph) in the 15-lap event, and won $6,300.

• 1978-1979 saw a new USSA three-race series called the World Series 600 Cross-Country. It was a circuit of 200 mile lake enduro events and had a 56 horsepower limit.

• Bob Elsner captured both the 340cc and the 440cc titles at the first Sno-Pro Race held in Sweden in 1978.

• In 1980 a *Race of the Relics* class was introduced at the Canadian Power Toboggan Championships in Beausejour, Manitoba for 1970 and older sleds.

• Feb. 20 & 21, 1982, Eagle River hosted its first 300 Lap Pro Enduro, sanctioned by MIRA

• February 1984 saw the running of the Green Lake Enduro Challenge featuring competition among antique snowmobiles. The antique sleds were ridden in competition against each other, using a handicap formula to equalize advantages.

• In 1990, Dave Wahl was the fastest driver in the Eagle River World Championship time trials and re-set the track record. His time of :36.62 seconds beat his 1989 time of :37.69.

URLs

World PowerSports Racing Association - **www.wpsaracing.com**
USSA Pro Star Racing Series - **www.ussaprostar.net**
Eagle River World Championship Derby Track - **www.derbytrack.com**
Pro Vintage Racing, Inc. - **www.provintageracing.com**
Canadian Power Toboggan Championships - **www.cptcracing.com**
International 500 Snowmobile Race - **www.i-500.com**
SnowRider online magazine - **www.snowridermag.com**
Snowmobile Hall of Fame and Museum - **www.snowmobilehalloffame.com**

Three sleds are racing for top position as they enter corner 3 here at Beausejour, Manitoba. The lead Ski-Doo is a 1978 Blizzard Super Stock, followed by a Polaris RXL. The Ski-Doo in the rear is a 1979 Super Stock, which is running next to a Mercury Sno-Twister.

Modern snowmobile oval racetracks are built by sprinkling thousands of gallons of water onto a prepared base, then letting the water freeze. This grader is keeping the track in top condition on race day. When the studded tracks of the snowmobiles race over the ice surface, it is broken up, creating a layer of ice crystals. As the layer becomes thicker and thicker, more of it is thrown up with each lap of a race into the faces of drivers. The grader comes out at regular intervals to completely clean the track, keeping it as safe as possible.

This photo is taken from a vantage point at the top of corner one-two on the Eagle River track, which as you can see from the width of the infield is a very sharp turn back into a straightaway.

This driver has lost control of her sled coming into corner three, so she, along with the machine, slid into the hay bales along the perimeter. Once the driver has reached a safe place, she gives the signal you see to show that she is all right, so the yellow flag can be lifted and racing can continue. At the finish of the race the machine will be removed from the track with a tow-sled.

This Twin Track Formula I SnoPro Racer is in the Snowmobile Hall of Fame Museum. It was owned and driven by Bob Anderson, driver #65. Anderson raced several different twin tracker models between 1986 and 1992. This sled is the one raced in February 1995, at the North American Championships in Antigo, Wisconsin—it was Anderson's last race before retiring. While driving Formula I Anderson won the Wisconsin State Championships twice.

Jim Adams, riding the #4 Ski-Doo, leads this very tight pack through corner three. Adams took home three 2004–2005 WSA Xtreme Ice titles—Stock 500, Stock 600, and the year-end points championship—to earn himself a place in the 2005 *Snow Week* Top 10 racer's list.

This sled is a 600 Polaris XCR Indy. Notice how the driver is in a full back steer as the snowmobile slides through the corner.

This photo was taken in the Snowmobile Hall of Fame Museum. The 1995 Polaris sled, #52, belonged to John Wicht III of Osseo, Minnesota, and was the machine that won the 1995 SOO I-500. Wicht, who drove the complete distance himself each time he entered, won the I-500 in 1988, 1992, 1993, as well as 1995. He was also the World Series of SnoCross Champion in 1992 and 1993.

This Ski-Doo is high siding, or his left ski is well above the ice. The rear of the sled is sliding out too far to make a smooth corner. This driver managed to avoid a crash by bringing the snowmobile back under control.

Chris Hortness on the Ski-Doo #17 leads through corner four in a heat race at the Eagle River World Championship week-end in 2003. He finished second in the World Championship that year behind teammate Jeremy Johnston. Hortness's sled had a Wahl chassis—some of the fastest in the racing world. The first ever Wahl race sled was built at the Arctic Cat factory in Thief River Falls in 1976. Dave Wahl attended an area vocational tech institute to learn welding, and spent his nights at Cat on his first self-built race sled. It was built from an original Wahl "straight axle" IFS front end construction, inspired from trying to reduce weight and improve the handling.

Jacques Villeneuve, #96, was the World Champion in 1980, 1982, and 1986. The 52 year-old "Flying French Canadian," won the Champ 440 title on the Eastern Pro Tour (EPT) for the 2004–2005 season. Villeneuve began his race career in 1973 wrenching and driving Alouette sleds with his brother Gilles, who died behind the wheel of a Ferrari in 1982 at the Dutch Grand Prix in Zolder.

P.J. Wandersheid, #28 (leading on the inside on his Arctic Cat), surprised oval racers by taking the Eagle River World Championship in 2002 as a rookie. Then, just to prove it hadn't been a fluke, he won it again the next year. He was also the 2003 Woody's Triple Crown Winner and 2003 WSA Pro Ice Overall Points Champion, as well as the *Snow Week* Racer of the Year in 2003. He races with the Wandersheid/AMSOIL Racing Team. His 2006 World Championship win at Eagle River made him one of only three racers to accomplish this feat.

Gary Moyle leads the field through corner three here. Thousands of spectators lined the ice oval at 3 p.m. sharp on Sunday, January 16, in Eagle River, Wisconsin for the Champ 440 class, to see who would take the 2005 World Championship. When the ice dust settled it was Gary Moyle for the checkered flag—and he also made it onto the *Snow Week* list of top drivers for 2005. Terry Wahl took second in the World Championship, with Dan Fenhaus earning third.

Dustin Wahl, #74, comes out of corner four in this photo. Growing up with Wahl Brothers Racing—home of the performance parts for performance people, Dustin is Dave Wahl's son and races under his dad's number. Dave Wahl won the Eagle River World Championship in 1990, riding with a broken ankle in an air cast. He was the fastest qualifier of the year, breaking the previous track speed record. Dave lead the championship for the entire race, leaving Eagle River with about $22,000 in prize money for the weekend, plus a new fur coat!

This photo of the Wahl Bros 1996 Super Sled Championships Twin Track Racer is taken in the Snowmobile Hall of Fame Museum. Driven by Terry Wahl, #47, this sled won the $50,000 Boswell Bonus, which was the largest purse in racing history, for winning 3 of 4 select races on the 1995–1996 race circuit.

Jacques Villeneuve, #96, leads in this race. Villeneuve set a record by taking the Toromont Cat Bonnechere Cup held annually in Eganville, Ontario, for the sixth time in February of 2005. It was the 31st anniversary of the country's second oldest snowmobile race. Villeneuve took the checkered for Ski-Doo at the hometown track in Valcourt in both 2005, and 2006, the 24th running of the Grand Prix de Valcourt.

Philip Moulton piloted a Wahl Chassis to win his first Champ 440 class in Beausejour, Manitoba, in 2005. The Champ 440 class is restricted to single track snowmobiles, so the twin track sleds popular a decade ago can't run here. Sleds must weigh a minimum of 350 pounds (159 kg). The brand of engine, hood, and logo must match, although any changes allowed in the Stock classes are permitted in the Champ 440 class.

Katie Olson drives Polaris sled #217, racing with her family out of Ramsey, Minnesota. Katie is the youngest; Heather Olson (#218) races Pro Women; while Glenn Olson (#219) rides in Super Senior. Katie was the Women's Amateur High Point Champion with the World Snowmobile Association Xtreme Ice Racing series in 2004–2005.

Brian Bewcyk, #39, from Winnipeg, Manitoba, races in the Pro Sprint classes, as well as the Pro Champ 440 and 600 classes. Bewcyk has won many races through his career, including some on the Eagle River Derby track—he took the checkered flag in the Pro Sprint 440/500 Darcy Ewing Memorial Race in 2003. Ewing was inducted into the Snowmobile Hall of Fame in 2006.

This Canadian Power Toboggan Championship heat race has two sleds racing through corner three. The #90 Artic Cat with its inside ski up off the ice is Johnny Kallock, who competes out of Alvarado, Minnesota. Behind him, the #69 driver, John Broermann from Sauk Center, Minnesota, is leaned into his turn.

This class of stock snowmobiles are packed tight during the first lap of their heat race on Beausejour, Manitoba's track. Notice that the headlights in the sleds are glowing in this picture—modified sleds generally do not run headlights.

Brian Bewcyk, #39, takes his share of the oval track out of the middle, in this spill in his Pro Sprint 500 heat race in Beausejour, Manitoba in 2004. Despite the accident Bewcyk had a great weekend, taking first place in Sunday's Pro Sprint 500 Final.

This heat race ended up with almost all Polaris sleds. The front sleds are throwing out a lot of snow, so visibility is reduced behind. In the World Snowmobile Association Xtreme Ice Racing Season Points finals in the 2004–2005 season, Polaris drivers took the championships in Junior 10–13, Junior Champ, Boys & Girls Junior 14–15, Junior 16–17 500, Masters, and all of the Semi-Pro classes.

The drivers in this stock class are running close as they take corner three. Stock sleds must run original OEM (or factory designated replacement) engines, tracks, skis, frames, cowls, suspensions and variable speed converters supplied by the manufacturer for the model used. Nothing may be removed from the sleds by means of heat, acid, drilling, grinding, sand blasting, peening, substitution, or any other means.

Joe Presta, Arctic Cat #80, drives out of Dryden, Ontario. Notice how much both he and Bewcyk, directly behind on the Ski-Doo, have leaned into the corner, while the driver to the left adopts a slightly different position.

Notice the sleds out in this ice oval don't look like the others in this section—you can see a lot of snowmobile track looking at the sleds. The reason is because these are actually snocross sleds competing in a special event at the 2003 Eagle River Derby weekend in Eagle River, Wisconsin, that did a specified number of laps on the snocross track, then matched that number going around the ice oval.

As sleds pull into their lanes at the start line, the ambulance waits trackside in case of an accident. Safety regulations require that an ambulance must be available before an oval race can run, so a race can't be resumed until a second ambulance arrives in the case of a driver being taken to a hospital.

Vintage oval classes like this one may run a variety of model years and styles, such as IFS and leaf-sprung, in a single class.

The first place sled in this vintage race clearly shows the spring stabilizer, which is added for ice oval racing to keep the ski and carbide flat on the ice.

This vintage oval class is competing towards the end of the day. The row of sleds running the center line are all following the groove that has been worn down over the day's racing. Corners can develop a large hollow that deepens over a weekend.

Chapter 3
EXTREME SPEED

Drag racing, also called straight-line racing, is the commonest form of snowmobile racing, practiced by everyone from backyard snowmobile tuning enthusiasts to pros competing on the same asphalt tracks as funny cars and dragsters. Likely the first race was a drag—and certainly there will never be a time when this highly competitive part of snowmobile racing loses popularity among participants. Drag racing is also the most versatile of the snowmobile events, taking place on all surfaces possible (drag racing on water is covered under watercross).

While the manufacturers spent the majority of their money promoting events like cross-country racing, oval sprint and enduro racing, and then snocross in the past, drag racing developed through the direction and commitment of thousands of race enthusiasts and small organizations across North America.

The Events

A drag race is defined as a straight-line acceleration event between two or more machines over a specified distance, where results are determined by order of finish. Speed runs, which use the same type of track, however, establish a winner by using individual timed runs.

Drag races on snow are the first and most common types of events. On modern race tracks snow drags are the entry point for drivers who want to try out racing or just performance test their sleds. Sleds generally launch off of a hard packed surface at a signal from the race starter and accelerate in a straight line for anywhere from 500 ft (152.4 meters) to 1,000 ft (30.5 meters), or up to a quarter of a mile (0.4 km).

One of the latest emerging types of drag racing on snow is hilldrags. They are held, as suggested by the

The driver on this 1000 cc modified Ski-Doo has just hit the trigger, lifting his skis slightly off the ground as the sled leaps forward. The driver leans ahead, his feet straight back, to help redistribute his own weight to keep the sled on the ice.

The drivers in this snow drag are participating in their first organized competition. The Ski-Doo in the foreground leaps off the ground—notice most of the track is also off the ground, so he doesn't launch nearly as quickly as the XCR Polaris sled in the background that is almost completely on the snow.

name, on hillcross tracks. Tracks are 500 ft (152.4 meters) long on groomed soft snow. The number of lanes is dictated by the hill characteristics, ranging from two to five. What makes this drag race exciting is that it is held on the steepest, smoothest part of the hillcross course—no jumps are included.

Also exciting, ice drags are the fastest form of winter drag racing. The surface is generally smooth natural ice that is well cleaned to allow traction products, or studs, to grip the ice. Race lengths vary. The speed reached is determined by the degree of modification on the sled and the types of fuels allowed by the class. Top speeds reached at the ISR World Series of Ice Drags in 2005 ranged from: Stock 440 at 90 mph (144 kph), Stock 700 at 100 mph (160 kph), to Open Mod 1000 at 131.55 mph (210.48 kph).

Grass and dirt (or turf) drags are the most popular form of summer snowmobile racing, with events scattered throughout the same area as the winter ones. Many racers participate year-round, so simply move from ice drags to grass drags once the snow disappears. Rules vary in grass drags depending on the class and organization. Grass drag top speeds range from an 800 A stock sled at 85 mph (136 kph), to a Lite Mod 1000 at 110 mph (176 kph).

The most prestigious form of drag racing is done on asphalt—it is also one of the most expensive areas of the sport to be involved in, since tracks are not readily available in small communities. Two organizations are important in asphalt drag racing: The National Snowmobile Drag Racing Association (NSDRA) and the National Speed Association (NSA).

This is the start of an ice drag race. All three drivers are poised, waiting for the lights in front of them to turn green and the race to begin. The same design as traffic lights, the light is red while the race is being set-up, and turns green when the starter or race director hits a switch.

Asphalt racing sleds use modified two and four-stroke engines adapted from all four major manufacturing lines, with a majority producing from 250 to over 300 horsepower. Many of the sleds hit speeds in excess of 150 mph (240 kph).

Speed runs are hosted at varying levels of competition, ranging from local enthusiasts running their sleds on a prepared surface and measured with radar guns or by local law enforcement, to organizations dedicated to that purpose, like the North Bay Snowmobile Speed Runs association (NBSSR). The track lengths vary, up to a distance of 2,000 ft (610 meters). Pro classes in the speed runs can top 150 mph (240 kph).

Vintage Drag Racing is one of the fastest growing events of the sport in some parts of North America. This type of event gives racers an opportunity to revive machines that may have been in storage for de-

cades and give them new life, while at the same time enjoying some winter competition themselves. The classes are usually set up with the ISR (International Snowmobile Racing) classifications that were used when the sleds first ran. The vintage machines also have plenty of speed and may hit 100 mph (160 kph) or more, depending on the class.

Driver Rules

Rules for drivers are established by individual governing bodies, affiliates, or associations, with the ISR (International Snowmobile Racing organization) rules being the standard. With hundreds of small local organizations, many of whom don't belong to the ISR, there are many variations in the application of rules across North America.

ISR rules require all drivers to wear safety equipment on the racetrack. The most important is a snell-approved full-face helmet, which must be securely fastened and worn even in the tune-up area. Upper body protection, a racing jacket, is required—motocross vests or hockey equipment do not meet the rules standards. Other mandatory items include: gloves, appropriate clothing, at least above ankle leather boots, shin and knee guards that cover from the instep to above the knee, and elbow pads are highly recommended. Eye protection is mandatory. Once dressed, the final thing the driver must wear in professional classes is a racing bib or other form of garment marked with their issued number.

Snowmobile Rules

The ISR rules have standards that are enforced in snowmobile grass and dirt drag racing, ice and snow drag racing, speed runs and asphalt racing, although some organizations expand and develop their own requirements in consultation with racers and membership.

The drag classes run numerous variations, ranging from Mountain Sled drag races, through Heavy Modified classes, to Stock, Improved Stock, and Pro Stock. Classes take into consideration combinations of all components on the machine including, but not limited to, model, weight, engine, chassis, and suspension to determine what is allowable, including fuels.

Basic safety rules set up by ISR standards include requirements for machine safety tether switches, the use of stands for clearing out tracks, and operational brakes. The more modifications made to the machine the more rules are enforced, such as all participants using external cooling systems (drag racing and speed runs) must use a catch pan to stop coolant from entering the environment when being used or disconnected.

The Evolution of Drag Racing

Drag racing happened everywhere—all over the country at many different winter festivals and snowmobile events. The first organized turf or grass drags, since they were unique however, drew more attention from the news media and interest from the factories. In 1966 and 1967 grass drags started as an interesting phenomenon to get spectators out to summer events. Some of the first included: Ishpeming, Michigan; Three Lakes, Wisconsin; and Blaine, Minnesota. Beausejour, Manitoba, held the first Canadian

Snowmobile Turf championships in November of 1968.

The big Beausejour championship provided an early opportunity for testing new Polaris TX models, so was well attended. The champion of the Super Elimination finals was local racer Clarence Baker, who beat John Sheedy and Ted Otto (who is well-known as a USSA Race Director), both riding the Polaris sleds.

By the next year Polaris jumped into the sport with a passion, using the grass drags to pave the way for winter sales. The summer of 1969 featured 13 grass drags from New York to Montana. In an overwhelming sweep, Leroy Lindblad took all of the modified classes at a rally aptly titled "Wish Winter" in Forest Lake, Minnesota. The open title at that grass drag race went to his teammate, Greg Grahn riding his Hirth Honker TX.

The USSA sanctioned its first summer grass drag race, billed as the World Championship of Summer Snowmobile Racing, at Three Lakes, Wisconsin, on July 1 and 2, in 1972. The track was an amazing eight-mile grass course, with a short woodchip sprint strip for the Sunday racing. They only held modified classes since they didn't have access to the classification information for manufacturer's new lines until the fall. Ed Schubitzke, with his Ski-Doo, took the Sunday Mod IV drag title. While participants and the 1,000 spectators enjoyed the event, the USSA decided to leave grass drags to smaller organizations due to the number of problems and low return for their investment.

This choice by the USSA shaped the future of drag racing to a great degree. Drag racers ended up with the advantage of having semi-professional and professional organizations that covered small geographic distances, so the expenses of the season's travel could be kept to a minimum. This, of course, increased participation.

Drag racing continued to grow over the next decade, with drivers experimenting more and more on different surfaces. A daring early asphalt racer was reported to have run on the Oxford Plains drag strip in July of 1985.

As well as not being limited to surface, drag racing, unlike other forms of snowmobile racing, gave women racers a distinct advantage—their small frames and light weights made it easier for them to excel than in many snow or oval events, where strength and stamina were key. Robin Dreeszen proved this

These two stock snowmobiles have just hit the trigger at the green light. Outdoor grass drag events are popular across North America as they provide great fund-raising opportunities for snowmobile clubs. Many of the clubs use the funds for their groomed trail system or other winter events.

by winning four Open Modified classes and posting the most wins at the Tombstone World Series of Drag Racing held in 1985. She was also named the ISR Drag Racing Driver of the Year.

Nineteen eighty-six was the sixth World Series of Drag Racing—held at Minocqua, Wisconsin, on an ice track. It attracted 506 entries, with racers competing for a $15,000 purse, including a Meyer Snow Plow, generators from Yamaha, as well as Yamabucks and Polaris Performance checks from the respective factories. Debbie Schmidt, from Rice Lake, took the Gold Medal in both the Open Mod 340 and 400 classes. Robin Dreeszen, won the heavy Mod 440, while Mike McArdle earned the 1986 high point championship.

Some of the grass drag cups won and defended in 1986 included the Michigan Cup, Condor Cup, and Vermont Championships. John Balley rode his Sell

Jamie Bellman drives the #303 Ski-Doo in asphalt drag racing. He captured his fourth career win at the Brainerd International Raceway in August of 2005, previously winning 1999, 2000, and 2004. His brother, and teammate, Bryan Bellman earned the 2005 high points championship with NSDRA.

Brothers Polaris to highest overall points to snatch the Michigan Cup from Greg McClain with his Polaris. Tom Lapointe defended his state title in Massachusetts to be the first to have his name engraved on the Condor Cup. It was the sixteenth annual running of the Kiwanis Club Grass Drags at Great Barrington, Massachusetts. Bob Pinto, riding his Mercury snowmobiles to victory, took seven classes at the Vermont State Grass Drags in Springfield, Vermont, on October 12. Tom Lapoint, the 1985 defending Champion, won the 650 Liquid Mod and Open Mod Liquid classes.

Drag racers Bryan Bellman and Pat Hauck both made the *Snow Week* list of 1990–1991 Drivers of the Year. Bellman finished the year with 32 first place finishes for an astonishing season on the ice. Hauck not only took home a good share of drag wins, but set NSSR speed records in IS8 and IS9 of 101 mph (161.6 kph).

Guy Parquette was named to the top 10 Racers of 1994–1995 by *Snow Week* after taking the winter Mini-World Series in Oconto Falls, Wisconsin and being the 1993–1994 *Snow Week* Racer of the Year. His great summer season on the grass drags was followed by a even better season on the ice. Unofficially, his title was "King of the Stocks" on his Ski-Doo racing sleds. Pat Salonek, who set 13 NSSR World Records during the same season, also made the list. His Mach Z ran in Improved Stock with a record speed of 119.008 mph (190.4 kph), while his improved MXZ hit 96.969 mph (154.7 kph).

The Wisconsin Cup of 1995 went to Craig Marchbank, who won classes in Stock, Improved Stock, and Pro Stock on board his modified grass drag Ski-Doos at Wausau. Pat Hauck, using pipes he'd developed himself—the Hauck Howlers—helped him win the High Points title in Improved Stock. Hauck's machine was a 1996 Vmax-4 800 that he'd bored up to a 900 cc powerhouse. Bill Bickford, another top driver, cleaned up the stock classes and some Improved Stock at the Snow Bash in Ohio, New York, on his Ski-Doo. Mike Nordstrum won four classes on his second day ever of grass drags (he was an ice racer and distributor for Bender Racing in Sweden) at the New York State Championship Drag Race in Cohocton. The Grassfire 500 at Red Creek, New York, featured Quebec's Rheaume Rodrique, a three time New York State Open Mod Champion, winning in the Heavy Mod 1000.

This speed run sled is housed in the Snowmobile Hall of Fame Museum in St. Germain, Wisconsin. It was driven by Jason Dunnigan, and owned by Jason and David Dunnigan. In September 2005, Jason Dunigan, of Jackson, Michigan, used his new sled to set a Pro Stock 1000 world record during the IHRA Amalie Oil North American Nationals at New England Dragway in Epping, New Hamshire. Dunigan ran 8.458 @ 154.09 mph (246.54 kph) during the first round of eliminations, which blew away both ends of the former PS1000 asphalt record. The team went on to back up their ET record by setting it even lower in the second round of eliminations to an outstanding 8.427.

Drag classes kept getting bigger and faster, and the first asphalt shoot-out was held in Brainerd, Wisconsin, in 1995. Like many snowmobile events, it began as an opportunity for the four manufacturers to showcase what their top sleds could do. Each manufacturer used Improved Stock 800s equipped with specially designed speed tracks and wheels built into the sled skis.

The roar of the engines and the smoke were commonplace to spectators at Brainerd's track, since the shoot-out had been added to the NHRA (National Hot Rod Association) event as a feature. When everything cleared, the Yamaha factory had taken the

A vintage Polaris TX-L is in the first lane in this snow drag race. This line of Polaris started as TX machines, then added the L for liquid cooled models. The number 55 sled is a Mercury Trail-Twister manufactured between 1973 and 1976. Sled #59 is a Yamaha.

This mod drag sled waiting at the start line shows all of the safety features required at a drag race. Notice the driver gear, including upper body protection and helmet. Also, the mechanic working on the sled has ear protection. The stand at the rear of the sled provides a safe enclosure for clearing the track or revving up the engine.

win, as sweet as it was, with driver Jerry Hauck taking his place in history as the winner of the first asphalt shootout.

Interest by speed lovers grew quickly, and the asphalt sleds were soon hitting speeds around 140 mph (224 kph) on Brainerd's incredible track. The 35,000 spectators had an opportunity to see what a snowmobile really could do. The NSSR (National Snowmobile Straightline Racing) asphalt world records in August of 1996 included the Open held by Dave Trygstad on a Ski-Doo at 9.817 ET. What exactly is ET? In E.T. Bracket Racing two vehicles of varying performance potentials can race on a potentially even basis. The anticipated elapsed times for each vehicle are compared, with the slower machine receiving a headstart equal to the difference of the two. With this system, virtually any two vehicles can be paired in a competitive drag race. Dan Coates held the Open speed on his Arctic Cat with 134.50 mph (215.2 kph).

In 1997, the NSSR took over the administration of the asphalt drags from the factories for the first time at the NHRA Nationals at Brainerd International Raceway. The line-up was based, instead of on manufacturer entries, on a points system that put the season's top drivers on the track. Changes continued and by 2001 there was lots of discussion as to why the factories seemed to be losing interest in asphalt drags after their early enthusiasm. Some pointed to the trail market change from triples to twins, so there was just less reason to support the models—while some said the factories needed head to head racing, or something the fans could understand, rather than the growing bracket racing.

Instead, the factory money seemed to be out on the grass drag drags in 2001. Polaris factory Team Red cleaned up in Aberdeen, South Dakota, with Chad Erlandson grabbing six first place finishes. Team Red chalked up another six firsts with clean sweeps in the Stock 600 and Improved Stock 600 at Viborg, South Dakota. By August they'd added another 53 first place finishes across the country. Ski-Doo also beefed up its grass drag efforts too, with a 25% increase in the program. With thirteen drivers covering the various different circuits their racers included pros like Craig Marchbank, Dave Vincent, and Guy Parquette. Snowmobile drag racing was coming of age.

Tina Duncanson was the drag racing driver on a hot streak in 2005. Piloting a Crooks/Wahl Brothers/Arctic Cat mod machine, she set a new record in the Top Gas class at the ISR World Series of Drags in Sault Ste. Marie, Ontario, February 18–20 with a 4.88-second elapsed time (ET) reaching 137 mph (219.2 kph). Winning all the way, she didn't even lose any of her heats.

Craig Marchbank also flew to victory—his twenty-three year career had been mostly on the grass.

Before a sled moves into its lane for an ice drag race, a team member clears loose snow and ice crystals off the track to provide the best traction for the sled's take-off. In the early years shop brooms were the tools of choice, but there are specialized sweepers available now to make this task more efficient.

Running Ski-Doo sleds (as many as 10 per raceday!) with the number 00, he was a master at fine-tuning and driving. Marchbank hit as many races in a year as possible, frequenting events sanctioned by the Pro Snowmobile Grass Drag Racing Association (PSGDRA), the National Snowmobile Racing Association (NSRA), and the Central Ontario Snowmobile Drag Racing Association (COSDRA). Ski-Doo's first sponsored grass drag racer, he always used Ski-Doo's latest models, so had a continual challenge to get something new figured out and into the winner's circle.

The winner's circle for Marchbank included being named *Snow Week's* Racer of the Year for 2005. How did a pro like Marchbank be so consistent for so long on the track? Well, he was one of those people who believed success is in the details, the very tiniest ones, so he completely disassembled every sled he raced and then put it back to together using the ISR rules for each class. That's dedication to the sport!

The sport of speed racing had lots going on track-side in 2005 too, with some great racing at the Central Minnesota Speed Association's (CMSA) February 26–27 event in Forest Lake, Minnesota. Kurt Mohawk, while he shot down a thousand feet to a top speed of 168.750 mph (270 kph) on his Anderson-based PSI Genesis 1620, didn't get to mark it as a record since it was his last race of the day, and he needed a second run within two percent of the record for it to make history—which he hadn't done in the earlier three tries. Mohawk did, however, set a CSMA World Record in Super Mod with a run of 162.711 mph (260.3 kph) and a backup time of 162.406 (259.9 kph). Marv Jorgenson also set a top speed of 167.117 mph (267.5 kph) in the Exhibition Class to take home some top honors for the weekend.

In other 2005 summer speed events, the organizers of the World Cup of Snowmobile Drags held annually in Fenwick, Ontario, ended their fifteen year tradition. Organizers, Henry and Stephen Bieda, cited declining returns as a key issue, along with politics. The drag site itself, however, seemed to have a new life

These two snow drag racers are using two different riding styles for controlling their sleds. If the driver requires more traction he stands closer to the rear of the sled. When the front end lifts more than he wants, a driver moves further ahead.

West Yellowstone, Montana, uses special starting lanes to help the snow drag sleds get better traction for their starts. Here, notice that old snowmobile tracks are cut in half and mounted on boards placed in each start lane. The driver positions the sled over the track so that when she hits the trigger the sled will have traction and take off, instead of spinning wildly as it normally does in soft snow.

beginning with an outdoor International ATV Expo. When one thing dies another often begins.

The US 131 Motorsports Park in Martin, Michigan, was the beginning of joint asphalt and drag racing for the NSCRA members. One of the memorable moments of the day included Dan Wade's run on his Jeff Simons owned Simon CPR turbo/nitrous Yamaha

RX-1. It became the first snowmobile to make a sub 8-second pass on a quarter-mile drag strip. The team recorded a fast time of 7.97 ET at 170 mph (272 kph).

The top-gun shootout at Tilbury, Ontario, put the fastest drivers and their teams up against one another for a weekend that hit the history books. Run by the Central Ontario Snowmobile Drag Racing Association (COSDRA), the Top-Gun Shootout offered lots of cash and bragging rights to its winners. The track itself was prime—a clay pad worked with rollers and a laser level until it was as smooth as a sheet of winter lake ice, in fact nothing short of outstanding.

Outstanding was a good word to describe the race events too, as the field narrowed to four machines in the King of the Trail class. Rob Shooping's Polaris lost to Phil Serra's Turbo RX-1, while Jerry Kaczanowski used his nitrous to defeat Dan Doddy's Arctic Cat. Serra ran a record-setting 4.72-second ET at 112 mph (179.2 kph). This COSDRA event was one of the season's most exciting.

Chris Anderson from Fenwick, Ontario, made season points at lots of grass drag races through the East coast and the Midwest. Among the many honors he took for the season, he earned top points in the North East Grass Drag Series in the Stock 900, 800, 800S, 600, and 600S classes! Named by *Snow Rider* as the top driver of 2004, he was honoured again by making the list of Top 10 in 2005.

Year-end awards honoured many speedy PRO (Powersled Racing Organization) grass drag racers for their 2005 season after their final event at Salisbury Center, New York. Danielle Meneely was voted driver of the year, honouring her achievement on the

This snow drag event is sanctioned by the SSRA (Saskatchewan Snowmobile Racing Association) in Fort Qu'Appelle, Saskatchewan. Here, driver #57, on the XCR Polaris, stands as far back as his arms will allow, on the running boards as he hits the trigger.

race track, which she balanced with collegiate studies. The high point winners included: Jared Hojnowski in stock, Jeff Detrick in Improved Stock, John Schneider in Pro Stock and Mod, and Wesley Kless in Juniors.

Indeed, the thrill-a-minute world of drag racing continued to prove that snowmobiles could go faster and faster, no matter what kind of track the sleds were on: asphalt, ice, or turf.

Memorable Moments of Speed

Speed was the ultimate goal in the 1970s—from the muscle cars on the highway, to the snowmobiles that hurtled down drag and speed run tracks. Specially built sleds, some that looked like a production snowmobile and others that barely resembled a snow machine, competed at different locations around the United States. The only problem was nobody recognized the records if they hadn't had anything to do with setting up the event, so everyone had to keep doing it over and over again.

Sled #242 in this vintage snow drag race is a 1979 Ski-Doo Citation. The sled in the middle is a Polaris, while an El Tigre is in the far lane.

This early 1970s sled is a Blue Max Speedway sled. The driver is wearing a vintage Mercury Sno-Twister suit.

This line-up of vintage drag race sleds has a Mercury Trail-Twister on the inside lane. A Ski-Doo RV is in lane two, with a TNT F/A (free air) in lane three. The SnoJet in lane four got the holeshot in this heat race.

Twenty different machines claimed at different times to have set the world speed records. They came out of various factories including: Ski-Doo, Mercury, Rupp, Alouette, Outboard Marine Corporation (OMC), Arctic Cat, Polaris, and the almost unheard of Sno-Pony.

The Rupp Super Sno-Sport looked like a rail dragster with its fuel-injected Ford V-8 engine in front of the driver, but qualified as a snowmobile with its tracks on short skid frames and skis on the front. It was, however, beaten at the March 1969 West Yellowstone Round Up that was sanctioned by the WSA (Western Snowmobile Assocation). Duane Eck took

the honors on his Ski-Doo Double Eagle, with its twin Rotax 669 engines under the bright yellow hood. He clocked a World Record of 95 mph (152 kph).

Early the next year, 1970, Ky Michaelson rode a rocket sled sponsored by Sno-Pony to a record 114 mph (182 kph) in Vermont. Nay-sayers refused to recognize this claim to fame, however, since the event hadn't been sanctioned. Instead Michaelson was invited to show up in West Yellowstone to compete with the latest everyone had to offer: The Polaris X-2 with a pair of 795 triples, a Mercury equipped with an outboard racing engine, and the first of Arctic Boss Cats, which was a twin-engined Panther built by Dale Cormican and driven by Roger Janssen.

At the close of the Yellowstone event Mike Baker drove away with the new world's speed record of 109.09 mph (174.54 kph) on the Polaris X-2. The machine acquired the nickname "the Flying Wedge" for its long blue shape. Dorothy Mercer took the honors for a women's world speed run on her Polaris as well, with a run of 107.01 mph (171.22 kph).

This time everybody got together and set a time and place for another speed run—Boonville, New York, February 1971. Arctic Cat had been turning daydreams into reality back in the plant after being whomped by Polaris the year before. The new Boss Cat was stylin' as they say. Building on the Polaris success, the Boss Cat had a 18 ft (5.5 meters) long wedge shape and a cockpit that looked like it was ready to fly overtop of a single 28 inch (71 cm) long track. The cowling covered a Kawasaki 800 cc engine from one of the King Cat oval sleds, plus a 1,000 horsepower turbine engine. This cat was definitely of the wild, untamed variety, even if it had skis. Unfortunately for its designers though, it wasn't quite ready for the racetrack.

Ski-Doo had brought its new twin-engined X-2R with Yvon DuHamel to drive it, but that soon fizzled out too, when it didn't run well either. Polaris was back and Mike Baker was anxious to get the record for them again, which he promptly went out and did. Baker broke his own record and set a new one of 118.11 mph (188.98 kph).

Not at all discouraged, Dale Cormican threw his fortune in with the Boss Cat and ran it two weeks later in Coon Rapids, Minnesota. It shattered the Boonville record with a speed of 125.87 mph (201.39 kph). Unfortunately for Cormican and Cat the run wasn't at any kind of sanctioned event, so it didn't hit the history books. That didn't stop Arctic Cat from doing their own promotion though, and sending the pretty purple Boss Cat around the country with flyers proclaiming it the fastest thing on snow.

The frenzy to go faster was just getting revved up. Alouette introduced Big Al, powered by four Kohler "Sunburst" free-air triples. The chrome sled made for excellent glossy photos and drew lots of crowds wherever it showed up, which after all, was what the whole thing was really about. The Ice Kutter, rumoured to be connected to Yamaha in some way, also appeared on the scene powered by a 455 Olds V-8, but never got any track time.

Wonder child of the Outboard Marine Corporation, the Johnson Pegasus, came out next to startle onlookers. Goodyear had even got involved in this one, specially molding the ultra-thin 15-inch (38 cm) wide involute drive track. This 14 ft (4.3 meters) long golden vision rode on bogie wheels, just like the OMC trail sleds. It was powered by two outboard 99.6 cubic-inch 2-stroke V-4 outboard racing engines. Running on pump gas and Johnson oil, the Pegasus reached a speed of 140.625 mph (225 kph) at the Boonville Track on August 19, 1971, but of course that wasn't a sanctioned event.

So, when Boonville rolled around for another "official" run at establishing a world speed record February 11, 1972 the snowmobile industry was standing by, holding its breath. USSA officials set up the rules and criteria to govern the event, so that the results wouldn't be disputable this time. Each machine had to make two runs past the official timing lights on the course—with the average of the two runs being the official time.

To make it fair, the USSA also set up a variety of classes for different engine sizes, including an unlimited class. The entries had to be snowmobiles of some sort, and USSA officials promptly proceeded to disqualify machines that didn't adhere to the basic mechanical principles of a snowmobile. So, the Sno-Pony was out without a chance to set any kind of record.

Cormican, with the Boss Cat I, ended up retiring from speed runs that weekend too in a blaze of—well, not glory. Ready for his first run, he hit the button to start the turbine, but when nothing happened, he hit it again. The explosion that followed ripped the big Boss Cat I into pieces and left Cormican in

A Mercury Sno-Twister, once known as the terror of B Stock classes, has the inside lane in the vintage snow drag race. They were produced from 1973 to 1976. Sled #220 in lane two is a Polaris.

a flaming wreckage—and needing a recovery of several weeks in the hospital.

Arctic Cat oval sprint racer, Charlie Lofton stepped up to strap himself into the Boss Cat II—although this time the Cat seemed to be losing its energy. Lofton's practice run, which didn't count, hit 139.2 mph (222.72 kph), while a second similar run, without his flameproof suit, didn't count either. The sled made one more run at 130 mph (206 kph), then burst a fuel line on the return trip, leaving Lofton with a low average speed.

Ski-Doo had two entries: the Inferno and the Ski-Doo X-2R. The Inferno was a rail-type dragster that promptly blew a track. The X-2R was an oversized Blizzard snowmobile powered by twin Rotax 766cc engines and piloted by Yvon DuHamel. The X-2R passed the timing lights at 129.2 miles (207.9 km) per hour, with its return run clocked at 125.4 (201.8 km), for an average run of 127.3 miles (204.87 km) per hour. In the end DuHamel ended up with a snowmobile speed record that would stand for five years as a USSA and a Guinness world record, until Donald J. Pitzen broke it with a speed of 135.93 miles (218.76 km) per hour on Union Lake in Michigan, February 3, 1977.

The Boss Cat II, undeterred, went on to claim two speed titles of its own: the NHRA (National Hot Rod Association) title at 130.05 mph (208 kph) and the WSA (Western Snowmobile Association) re-

The #819 Rolloflex is in the first lane. Rolloflex were built between 1971 and 1974. The Yamaha has a narrow lead in the first sled lengths of this vintage race. An Alouette 340 Super Brute got a poor start in lane three, while the #257 SnoJet Astrojet in lane four is closing in on the leader.

cord at 123 mph (196.8 kph). By the next fall, however, the fuel crisis hit the snowmobile racing world and the speed wars quietly came to an end. The Boss Cat II was beautifully restored by the Jim Warning family of New Lenox, Illinois, and was added to the Hall of Fame Museum.

Who's in the Hall of Fame from Drag Racing and Speed Runs?

The drag race has always been recognized as the best way to compete to establish the maximum speed of a snowmobile, so speed runs have played an important part in the development of the industry.

Cormican, Dale – Inducted 1997. Raced Arctic Cat.

Earhart, Tom – Inducted in 1994. Raced Rupp, Speedway, Polaris, and Arctic Cat.

Eck, Duane – Inducted in 1990. Rode Ski-Doo, Arctic Cat, and Polaris.

Jorgenson, Marv – Inducted in 2002. Rode Kawasaki, Mercury, and Polaris.

Lofton, Charlie – Inducted in 1991. Raced Arctic Cat

Mercer, Dorothy – Inducted in 1993. Raced Polaris.

Muetz, Gordy – Inducted in 2001. Rode Yamaha.

Nelson, Brian – Inducted in 2000. Rode Polaris, Ski-Doo, Arctic Cat, and John Deere.

Mercer, Dorothy – Inducted in 1993. Raced Polaris.

Schlueter, Perry – Inducted in 2001. Raced Yamaha.

The background sleds have trackside seats as their ancestors take to the racetrack once again three decades after they hit the snow. The #809 sled in lane one is an SS-300 Skiroule. Lane two has an Arctic Cat Lynx, while the lead sled is an Artic Cat Puma.

DRAG RACING'S AMAZING FACTS:

• The first annual World Championship Snowmobile Pull was held in Danville, Indiana, September 14, 1980. Stan Hughes' stock Arctic Cat pulled 4,590 pounds (2082 kg) the full 200 ft (61 m). There were 80 contestants, with all of the championships won by Arctic Cat drivers.

• The Pigeon Hills Snowmobile Club hosted the first ever Mason-Dixon Grass Drags two miles south of the Pennsylvania/Maryland border on November 20, 1983. Nearly 60 sleds and more than 300 spectators were there to witness the North beat the South 8-4.

• Marv Jorgenson rocketed his Chopper City racer to a world record speed of 158.53 mph (253.6 kph) on February 3, 1985 at the St. Paul, Minnesota, Budweister/Saint Paul Winter Carnival Speed Run on Lake Phalen.

• Tom Earhart broke the National Snowmobile Speed record four times. His final season of speed run competitions he posted a top speed of 177.04 mph with the Arctic Cat Silver Bullet in 1986.

• 1986 saw the formation of the first speed run organization. The National Snowmobile Speed Run (NSSR) created uniform rules, tech inspection, track length and promotion.

• Mike Knapp broke the 9-second barrier in asphalt drags with his Yamaha Vmax-4 800 down a quarter mile track in 8.84 seconds at 146 mph (233.6 kph), on a practice run in Brainerd in August 2001. Knapp had already amassed 17 titles in his career at the World Series of Ice Drags.

• March 14, 2005, was a record breaking weekend on the NBSSR track in North Bay, Wisconsin. Chris Hanson, of Team Anderson, set a new Guinness record for the world's fastest single engine sled at 173.2 mph (277.12 kph). They also broke the previous world's record with their nitrous oxide machine, Modzilla, with a run of 192.2 mph (307.5 kph).

• The top speed at the 2005 ISR World Series Ice Drags in Sault Ste. Marie, Ontario, was 137 mph (219.2 kph), recorded by Tina Duncanson of Acton, Ontario, in the Heavy Mod 1000 class, on an Arctic Cat.

URLS

National Snowmobile Drag Racing Association - **www.nsdra.org**
National Snowmobile Racing Association - **www.nsraracing.org**
The Central Ontario Snowmobile Drag Racing Association - **www.cosdra.com**
The Central Minnesota Speed Association - **www.cmsaracing.com**
Rebelsled information on more than a dozen drag racing circuits - **www.rebelsled.com/Associations.htm**
National Speed Association - **www.nationalspeedassociation.com**
SnowRider online magazine - www.snowridermag.com
Snowmobile Hall of Fame and Museum - **www.snowmobilehalloffame.com**

This is the start of a grass drag and the two sleds have just passed the light standard. Lights are mounted on a pole in the middle of the track. The Race Director or starter holds the electronic device that will turn the light green once all of the drivers are ready for the race to begin.

Competition is keen as these three sleds get an almost equal start on the turf at the annual Sintaluta Grass Drags event in Saskatchewan. Drivers set up their sleds to suit their own styles, with the Formula Ski-Doo rider squatting over the back of his seat, while the next Ski-Doo driver stands on the running boards and leans ahead.

Notice the poles and wires that separate each of these two sleds race lanes. Modern drag racing associations usually use electronic equipment like this to make sure drivers don't jump the green light.

The rules for modified sleds in grass drags may not require that they run with hoods. Cooling is a problem for sleds running in the heat, so auxiliary cooling systems are used to bring the engine temperature down once the race is over.

Studs are installed in drag sled tracks in many classes, particularly on the ice and grass, to provide for a good "hook up" of the snowmobile track with the racing surface. The pattern or frequency of installing the studs is determined by the driver and his mechanic. Various lengths of studs are available, and drivers must follow the rules of their association or they will be disqualified.

Pit crew members are important in all forms of racing. This crewman is using a steel blade to scrape the ice as smooth as possible to ensure the sled will have good traction. Studs chip the ice away as the track spins when the racer hits the throttle, so each time a machine goes through the lane it must be carefully examined and cleaned by the next crew.

DUNIGAN RACING

1000 CC Top Gas

DRIVER: Jason Dunigan
OWNER: Jason & David Dunigan
CREW: David Dunigan, Paul Austin, Nate LeFer
CHASSIS: Bowen Chassis
ENGINE: Polar Performance Steve Payne
CLUTCH: HRP Motorsports Brad Hulings
PAINT: HCP Designs Chad Harris
SET UP: Paul Austin
SPONSORS: Wiseco, Cometic, HRP Mortosports Woodys, Polar Performance, Race Pax JAWS Performance, Paul Austin Racing
IGNITION: MSD
TRACTION: Woody's Traction Products

This Dunigan Racing sled in the Snowmobile Hall of Fame Museum is a 1000 cc Top Gas racer. Each part of the sled was hand-built. The chassis was by Bowen Chassis; the engine from Polar Performance engineer Steve Payne; the clutch was from Brad Hulings at HRP Motorsports; and the set-up was by Paul Austin.

The Arctic Cat El Tigre in lane one of this vintage snow drag starts off the line with its running boards nearly touching the snow. The reason for this is that early model sleds didn't have a tapered tunnel so that the rear of the running boards started out a lot closer to the ground. The #336 sled is an Arctic Cat Puma.

This ice drag racer is on his 600 Ski-Doo. Notice how the mod drag sleds use the short skis like an oval racing sled. Carbides are attached to the underside of the ski for responsive steering on the ice.

This is the staging area of a snow drag race—the lanes are in the background of the picture between the posts. Notice several different types of snowmobile stands, which have been brought ahead for drivers moving their machines. The vertical plywood sheets stop the debris from flying into staging. Sheets of plywood are also used as the "Boards" that advise racers who placed in the heats and when their next races run. Snow drag event organizers often do not have sound systems, so the Boards are used to keep the race running smoothly.

This sled shows how packed an asphalt racer is under the hood! The #387 sled is driven by Rich Stumpf on both the NSDRA and NHRA circuits. This Arctic Cat puts out about 285 hp and 155 pound-feet of torque. It's a Trygstad built 1006 cc engine with an Artic Cat case and crank, cylinders and 52 mm carbs from the Crank Shop and Jaws pipe. Underneath is a 136-inch Wahl chassis and suspension.

This photo shows a highly competitive class, as three grass drag-gers are several sled lengths away from the start line already and still fairly even. The turf has been ripped up through the day by the studded tracks, so there's a lot of black dirt flying out the rear of each sled.

This drag race has four sleds across the field, just passing the starter who is standing behind a straw bale between lanes two and three. When the sleds are lined up in order at the start line the start-er gets a nod from each racer in turn, signifying that they are ready for the race to begin. Once the racer in lane four has nodded, the starter presses the button that will turn the lights from red to green, so the race begins.

This North Dakota racer uses a special harness to allow him to compete in drag races with his snowmobile. Born without legs, he is still able to participate in this exciting sport thanks to the innovations of his crew.

Take a close-up look at this part of what's under the hood on an asphalt race sled, such as the MSD high performance ignition; the coolant lines and surge tank with quick couplers to connect to the external cooling system.

The kids on the 120 minis also get to participate in grass drag racing. Their sleds are equipped with wheels, either instead of skis or attached to the ski assembly.

Notice the left ski on this grass drag sled—the ski hoop is covered with duct tape. The duct tape ensures that the snowmobile will trip the timer in its lane at the end of the race track. Without the tape the electronic system may miss tripping at the ski tip, catching the sled only when the hood passes. Since drag race finishes can be very close this is extremely important.

These three snow draggers are still even a sled length from the start line. Sleds are currently classified according to engine size. This is a Stock 800 class, so the machines are allowed to have an engine capacity up to 800 cc, although drivers can also up-class, or take a sled with a lower engine capacity into any stock class above it.

This driver is cleaning his grass drag lane with a sweeper. A driver can start at any place within his lane, so he first inspects the area to determine if hollows have been dug into the turf that would reduce traction, then cleans the area under where his machine will sit, along with a sled length or two in front of the machine.

One of the race sleds in the Snowmobile Hall of Fame Museum, this drag sled was driven by Jerry Solem of Minocqua, Wisconsin. It won four World Championships: Rice Lake, Minocqua and Riverton, Wisconsin; and Cedarville, Michigan, in Improved Stock, Pro Stock, and Factory Mod classes. The motor is a Polaris Indy 650 bored out to 700 cc (3 cylinders).

This photo shows the cooling lines that are attached to Jerry Solem's drag sled in the Snowmobile Hall of Fame Museum. Specialized drag sleds do not have a radiator, but are cooled after each race by having water pumped through the cooling system from a cool down cart.

Ron Bray of Bray Racing drives this asphalt sled. Notice the long body and track—asphalt sleds must weight at least 650 pounds (295.45 kg) with a driver and fuel. All asphalt race sleds must have a minimum 1-inch (2.54 cm) of travel in the track suspension. Only steel springs are permitted, with externally activated suspension systems prohibited. Hyfax must be removed. Bogie wheels must be used on each side of the rear suspension to keep the slide rails from coming in contact with the rubber track surface.

The photo shows the skis used on the asphalt racetracks. The minimum length for skis is 15 inches (38.1 cm) and the maximum length is 21 inches (78.74 cm). Both skis must be identical and not staggered on the snowmobile. The skis, along with a specially made Camoplast challenger track, are the key changes mechanics make to their stock sleds to try out asphalt racing. Before manufacturers began to create products especially for this part of the sport, drivers used a regular track and rollerblade wheels mounted inside a set of regular skis.

The Ski-Doo shown here is owned and driven by Ted Wiegle in asphalt racing. Notice how low the sled sits to the ground, a mere inch or two off the asphalt. Mechanics do this for three reasons: to lower the center of gravity, making weight transfer less dramatic; to reduce the front "profile" of the sled, thus making it more aerodynamic; and to reduce the approach angle of the front of the skid/track, which reduces the friction of the track rolling around the skid.

Darrin Weber drives the #533 Polaris asphalt racing sled. Notice how low the front profile, or "frontal area" is on this sled, which results in a reduction in aerodynamic drag. Some simple changes help reduce drag, such as the low profile windshield. When racing, the driver crouches down behind the windshield, with his elbows tucked inside the front profile too.

This photo illustrates some of the things an asphalt driver can monitor during the few seconds a race takes. One of the most important asphalt racetracks—and the location of the first large asphalt race—is the Brainerd International Raceway (BIR). It is a multipurpose racing facility located on a 400-acre site in central Minnesota north of Brainerd, near North Long Lake. BIR was originally known as Donnybrooke Speedway when it opened in 1963, but the name was changed with its sale in 1973.

Chapter 4
EXTREME WATERCROSS

Snowmobile watercross is the least well-known of the snowmobile sports—and it isn't because it's new or not exciting! In fact, watching sleds zip across the water, while you're relaxing on green, grassy shores, is one of the best times to be a spectator at a snowmobile event. And there's lots to see, because as drivers say, "If you're not sinking, you're not racing."

The Events

Early watercrossers determined only limited changes needed to be made to successfully get up on top of the water. Speed was the single factor in floating instead of sinking, along with a rich fuel mixture to prevent the engine from overheating. They also made adjustments to create the maximum distance between the chassis and track, reducing water build-up that would make the sled heavier and harder to turn. So, with few machine changes, and some daring individuals, a new sport was born.

Watercross drag racing is the usual entry point for drivers getting established in competitive snowmobile racing on the water. The racer launches on one side of a water body to shoot straight across to a landing site, so he can perfect the machine's ability to stay on top of the water before attempting to turn. Heats of three or four drivers are run, with the first driver to the finish line, which is some feet from shore, declared the winner.

Matt Ledin, driver #78 makes a turn with his Polaris watercross sled at the World Championship Snowmobile Watercross event in Grantsburg, Wisconsin.

Pro Open racer, Scott Mosher, takes the lead around the buoy on his #34 Polaris sled. These drivers made a straight shot from the beach onto the race track, then turned to the right onto the oval course, continuing to make right turns throughout.

Oval sprint racing on water is the more exciting of the two events. Buoys, which racers must keep outside, are used to mark the track. Three or four racers start from a launch site or start point on the beach and make their way onto the water to begin the oval. Feature Finals can have more machines on the water, with the additional sleds starting two seconds later from a back row. A race usually consists of three or more laps, at the discretion of the race officials. The finish line is on the straightaway back to the start point on the beach, once the final buoy has been rounded.

Driver Rules

Rules for drivers are established by the IWA (International Watercross Association) and ISR (International Snowmobile Racing). Drivers are required to wear safety gear. This includes, as in all forms of racing, a full-face helmet with a SNELL approval. Helmets must be bright colors, although blaze orange

Semi-Pro Stock oval racer Larry Lange, #181, takes his Ski-Doo over the course. A watercross sled must maintain a high enough speed to keep on top of the water, so high horsepower engines are required.

These watercross drag races have just launched from the beach and are headed straight ahead to the opposite side of Memory Lake in Grantsburg, Wisconsin. There are generally four start lanes, although some race locations or classes may run additional sleds for a feature race, which are in a second row that is started a few seconds after the first row.

isn't required. Drivers must wear an U.S.L.G. (or Canadian equivalent) approved 100 mph rated life vest of any bright color. Clothing must completely cover the body, including shoes and socks and shirts. Motocross style pants are required in Oval and Mod Drag classes. As with all other areas of snowmobile racing, eye protection is required for everyone in the staging and starting line areas. It is recommended that those in the pit or paddock area wear eye protection at all times as well.

Driver classes have two age categories: general and veteran's oval (driver must be over 40 years of age). In ovals, drivers race as either semi-pro or pro, taking experience into consideration.

Snowmobile Rules

The snowmobile used in watercross must be an actual full body snowmobile consisting of standard snowmobile parts including: track, chassis and belly pan, skis, centrifugal snowmobile clutches, and all other parts. The seat may be removed. Driver numbers in watercross must be affixed to the belly pan as well as both sides of the hood.

Snowmobiles don't use any floatation devices to help them stay on top of the water, although a cushion may be used as a seat. The following are not allowed: studs or traction devices on the track; rudders (any type of device that attaches to the snowmobile and rides in the water at any time); or airfoils (Any type of device other than a standard hood that attaches to the snowmobile with the primary function of altering the flow of air around the snowmobile). The machines may burn pump fuel, but race fuels are recommended. Any fuels used may be tested for water solubility and other elements. Machines must have biodegradable chain case oil and antifreeze. Nitrous oxide, turbo charges, and pressurized fuel tanks are not allowed.

All other machine adjustments and changes are regulated by the rules for the individual classes on the drag and oval racetrack.

The Evolution of Watercross

The first snowmobilers who tackled the open water were a group of New Hampshire fun-seekers in Canterbury. The Sno-Shaker club held their first event in 1975, and went on to hold a Second Annual Snowmobile Water Ride in 1976. Organizers were quick to point out that their event was for fun and not something the average rider would want to do. There were, however, some who thought the techniques could be useful if applied to trail riding and unfortunate encounters with open water.

Serious snowmobile watercross racing was born the following year in the village of Grantsburg, Wisconsin, in 1977. It started as a dare between snowmobilers and grew into a World Championship of Watercross series that has lasted thirty years.

The Grantsburg races are held on Memory Lake, which is a small flowage created by a dam on the Wood River. Its size and depth are perfect, so all a driver has to do is stand up when he sinks and the sleds are easily located and retrieved. Located a block from downtown Grantsburg, all services are nearby. Local promoters at some point dubbed the event the "Fastest Show on H2O" and summer watercross grew.

With Memory Lake as a backyard, local racer Mark Maki became the watercross driver to beat. He progressed rapidly from a straight shoot-out, just to get across, to being able to turn and run an oval race around the lake. His early records started at: 3,000 ft (915 meters) or 0.5 miles (0.8 km), then a 2.5 mile (4 km) straight ahead shoot across the larger Yellow Lake.

Watercross spread quickly to nearby communities. On October 6, 1979, at Yellow Lake, Maki set a new oval record that shattered all earlier attempts. Riding his Ski-Doo 7500 Blizzard, he went a grand total of 11 miles (17.6 km) before running out of gas and plunging into the cool water. Other competitors that day included Wayne Tonn, Dennis Gauthier, Dale Soderbeck, and Scot Maki, with the longest of their runs short of 3 miles (4.8 km). Mark Maki continued to set records, with one of 67 miles (107.2 km) lasting for years.

Henry Beida, a Ski-Doo snowmobile dealer from 1974, rose to a challenge that would earn him—well not fame and fortune—but two unofficial records, which still stand in professional snowmobile circles. The first was a gruelling 32 mile (51.2 km) trip across the waves of Lake Ontario, on August 20, 1988. Considering the lake is the world's fourteenth largest, with a maximum depth of 802 ft (244 m), Beida was gambling the cost of his 1985 Ski-doo Formula SS if it sank. The size also makes it the largest body of water ever crossed by a snowmobile.

Beida worked on his sled for some time before he made the run, changing its stock engine for a 1983 Rotax 521cc engine. He arranged a support boat with Captain Chris Hemmingway, Bart Greer, the Ontario Provincial Police, and the Canada Coast Guard. The ride, which went from Port Dalhousie to Toronto Island, took just 42 minutes for an average speed of 45.6 mph (73 kph).

Going one further, Beida also set a new unofficial watercross record June 9, 1989, on Old Welland Canal, Welland, Ontario. This time he upgraded the 1985 Ski-doo Formula SS with a 1989 Rotax 580 cc engine. He went 100.1 miles (160.16 km) in just over nine consecutive laps on the 11.1-mile (17.76 km) course. The record setting attempt ended after 1 hour and 42 minutes when the machine sank, out of gas at the starting line. He had averaged 58.8 mph (94 kph).

So why are Beida's records unofficial? He submitted all of the substantiating documentation to the Guiness Book of World Records as required, only to be advised that they were not currently accepting snowmobile distance records in any other area than distance travelled over snow.

At the same time Beida was setting watercross records, the International Watercross Association (IWA) was created. The organization began in 1989 to develop rules to guide and control watercross racing events, and enforce those rules to ensure fair competition. Drivers involved in Watercross came from Wisconsin, Minnesota, Michigan, Indiana, Illinois, Ohio, Iowa, Pennsylvania, New York, and Canada. For the 2001 season the IWA merged with the WSA to become WSA Watercross, which changed name again in late 2005 to become WPSA Watercross.

Mark Maki continued to dominate watercross, proving to be a true professional master. By 1997 Maki had collected 11 Grantsburg World Championship wins and 10 IWA World Series high points titles on his Ski-Doos. The first Arctic Cat to ever take the World Series, driven by Dale Lindbeck, had been the previous year in 1996, which Maki promptly captured back. As more and more drivers entered the competition—192 registered for the 1997 Grantsburg event—there were lots of sleds from every manufacturer. The 1998 year end points had a driver from each brand in the top four of the Chopper City Pro

This Ski-Doo driver is wearing all of the required safety gear and clothing that completely covers his body. He is not racing in this photo, but crossing the lake to the pit or paddock area after his run.

Oval class: Maki first on Ski-Doo; Mike Roe second on Polaris; Kevin Gibbs third on Arctic Cat; and Jeff Fischer fourth on Yamaha.

The 2001 watercross season showed a lot of new names—and some old ones—were taking it to the limits on the water. Dale Lindbeck's Arctic Cat narrowly captured the World Championship from defending champion, Yamaha driver Jeff Fischer, taking the lead on the last lap. Driving a Jaws Performance race-prepped Ski-Doo, Tadd Fredrick won the Mod 700 drags the same weekend. Phil Cashman, took the Pro Stock Oval classes in both the Wild Rose, Wisconsin, race and the Grantsburg World series. In sleds, Scott Stanczak was taking a unique RMI mountain sled around the buoys at Grantsburg. Jeff Moyle made his first Pro Open win at the Wild Rose with his Polaris Indy 700 Pro X.

Watercross kept getting hotter and hotter, with the 2005 World Series of Watercross in Grantsburg, Wisconsin, on July 15–17, a real scorcher—on and off the track. With temperatures soaring to the 100 (37.7 C) plus mark, a dunk in Memory Lake seemed rather like a good thing—unless of course, you were one of the drivers.

Besides trackside there were a few very popular spots in Grantsburg that weekend: the lemonade stand and the misting station, where red-hot bodies lined up for a little relief from the heat. Even the thousands of campers, who trekked annually to Grantsburg for the whole weekend, got little relief as nights stayed hot.

It was an event well worth a little sunburn, as the racing was superb. Rookie Chad Maki was a crowd favorite, following in dad Mark Maki's footsteps—or ski marks, as the case may be.

Notice how this sled adheres to the rules and displays its driver number on the bellypan—it's easy to see why when you can see the sleds in action. Sled #812 is driven in the Pro Veteran Oval class by Dennis Rhyner.

These four sleds are lined up at the starting line under their respective lane numbers. Notice that there is only a sled length of sandy beach before they will hit the water after accelerating when the start flag drops. In the early days of watercross sleds were given a much longer run to the water to build up speed.

First taking the Stock Drag 800 class, young Maki (just fourteen) proceeded to show everyone he could turn circles just as good as his dad too. When the green flag dropped on the Semi-Pro Stock Oval he hit the first buoy in the lead. While he had to dodge sunken drivers on the next laps, he never once wavered. Mitch Allen finished in second place behind him.

It looked for awhile like Dale Lindbeck might end up with second in the 8-lap Pro Open when his Arctic Cat took Busse out for second when he went to the equalizer buoy, then squared Nelson off on the inside line when he made his late-race move to the equalizer buoy on lap six. Lindbeck was in the lead, but could he keep it?

Nelson, despite his best efforts, ended up losing to the lake, and went down in Lindbeck's wake. Lindbeck took the checkered flag for his third Grantsburg title, repeating his 1996 and 2001 victories. Second place went to Andy Busse, and third to Loren Ward on his Polaris.

Loren Ward's season was just getting rolling at Grantsburg, however, and he had plenty more glory ahead of him. He stole the show at the Flat Rock Watercross in Lowville, New York, on August 13–14, 2005. Taking three firsts in Pro Ovals and two seconds, his Polaris was performing well.

While the Flat Rock watercross drags had never been won by anything but a Ski-Doo or Polaris,

Shawn Zurn, #76, rides this Polaris snowmobile in watercross racing. The large orange buoy marks the course. On at least one lap of the race each driver must go around an equalizer buoy on a far outside line. This rule is designed to level the playing field.

Jim Seese changed all that by winning the Semi-Pro Stock 700 event on both days with his Arctic Cat. Seese also took his sled out on the snow and water, so he made the most of the seasons.

As the racing season continued, Dale Lindbeck came out on top again in the Pro Open at the fourth annual watercross in Frederic, Wisconsin. It seemed his Arctic Cat was unstoppable, grabbing first place in the points—a feat he did for a third time in Hill City at WPSA's Park X.

However, three wins weren't enough to cinch the Pro Open championship. Andy Busse managed to grab that position at the last race of the season October 1–2 in McHenry, Illinois. Busse also captured the season points championship in the Pro Stock ovals. Young Chad Maki rode to the high points in his two classes too: Stock 800 Drags and Semi-Pro Stock Ovals.

Watercross drivers in the Eastern part of the country also had a great year. The Fremont, New Hampshire race, where drivers also had their annual East/West Challenge race had some excellent racing action. Scott Mosher took the 600 Pro Open ovals, while Scott Hunt scooped the win in the 800 Pro Ovals. Fremont's track is unique in that the oval sleds race around an island, so the only buoys on the course were to mark the inside line and the outside, equalizer line.

With so much enthusiasm for the sport it's certain that as long as summers are sunny and hot, snowmobilers will be taking their sleds over the water.

Memorable Moments in Watercross History

The day of the Second Annual Snowmobile Water Ride, September 12, 1976, dawned bright and sunny in Canterbury, New Hampshire. Over 2,000 people, anxious for the event to begin, gathered on the shores of the rather ordinary looking slough that took up a portion of an ordinary farmer's field.

Meanwhile, the drivers were having the usual meeting—although for many of these 45 racers it was the first they'd ever attended. Carl Peterson, race director (and proprietor of the nearby Canterbury village General Store) conducted the meeting. One of the first to prove to the Sno-Shakers club the year previously that 600 pounds (272.7 kg) of man and machine truly could skim across the water, Peterson was giving hints to ensure a great day for the crowd.

While a few last minute riders were unloading their sleds and throwing down their $2 fees, the majority headed out to walk the track. The water body itself was 230 ft (70 m) long, 8 ft (2.4 m) at its deepest point, so sinking would be serious. A 400 ft (121.9 m) approach, covered with fresh mown hay, led down to the water's edge, allowing for an ample run.

Bright orange flags straddled the approach to the water, while a ribbon covered pole marked the target on the opposite side—the exit. But there was more than making it across at stake here. Indeed, the contest required some finesse, since judges were looking at elapsed time and smoothness of the ride. And, just to make sure everyone felt challenged, all riders who successfully made the drag race across the pond were eligible for two tries at making a right-hand turn around a buoy in the middle of the pond—high points there went to the sharpest turn.

But what if they still wanted more? Well, all drivers who made it through the first tests of skill on the water became eligible for two tries at clearing a 10 inch (25.4 cm) high wooden jump (similar to a waterski jump) situated 15 ft (4.6 m) from shore, then making it all the way to the far shore still 200 ft (61 m) away.

Drivers prepared their sleds—after all most had been hurriedly dragged from the garage in whatever condition they'd been parked when the snow melted. Most tied up or removed their tail flaps so water could flow more easily around the track. A few cautious drivers taped or covered the forward air vents with cardboard so water wouldn't spray the belt or soak the clutch. Air intakes under the cowling were turned to face backwards. Modifications done, the race director called drivers to line up.

The contest was ready to begin!

Skip Ladd put on his helmet and lifebelt, then proceeded to get the watercrossing gear attached to his Scorpion Whip 440. He tied a long rope to his ski tips—just in case—and looped it over his seat, then looped a tether cord attached to a "kill button" around his right wrist. He was ready.

Two thousand people all stopped breathing.

Every driver on the track knew exactly what was required to make it over that shimmering body of water. Speed. Speed. And more speed. Ladd wound up his sled; 20 mph, 30 mph, hitting the slough full-tilt at 45 mph. He was literally flying with the water as smooth as glass beneath him.

He pulled the sled up on the opposite shore and turned back to the crowd. A victory cheer—the first of many, rippled along the racecourse. More than one-third of the 45 drivers cruised over the water to qualify for round two and the tougher challenge.

The successful drivers demonstrated a simple strategy: Make sure the sled's approach was absolutely straight, sitting far to the rear of the sled to raise the skis and keep the nose high, but immediately pressing down on the nose when they hit the water. In the more than 100 tries at the water not a single snowmobile crashed abruptly or threw a rider. Instead the sinkers simply ran out of momentum and dug themselves into the water.

This Ski-Doo watercross sled is in the Snowmobile Hall of Fame Museum, on loan from Mark Maki. Maki had the most impact on watercross racing of anyone in the industry—he holds twelve World Championship Watercross titles. He resides in Inver Grove Heights, Minnesota.

Experiences were varied, as lots of drivers emerged with dry clothes, and a few others learned how to start their sleds after being "drowned," a feat which proved easier than many expected. Even the most difficult to start had only taken half an hour, which wasn't a lot different than some cold winter mornings.

Winners? Skip Ladd, first on the water, also walked away with the water ride portion of the event, clearing the 230 ft (70 m) pond in four seconds. After the Whip's impressive run, Ladd loaned it to Dick Wheeler, whose bravado earned him a victory in the water jump with 4.5 seconds. Vern Smith won the turning competition with his SnoJet.

The water ride event was the first of many similar ones held formally and informally across North America for the next thirty years, whenever a few snowmobilers got the urge to run their machines on a hot summer day.

Driver #991, John Fleischman, takes a dunk in Memory Lake with his Arctic Cat in his Semi Pro Open heat race. Notice his right hand—he has just pulled the tether switch, so his sled didn't go down running and damage the engine.

WATERCROSS RACING'S AMAZING FACTS:

• Aug. 21, 1983 Greg "Jaws" Balachin of Ontario was named the new World Champion of Watercross with 89 points in the four race series. He was nicknamed "Jaws" due to the extended nose he attached to the front of his 1978 Ski-Doo RV.

• The first Victor Ford Challenge ran in McHenry, Illinois on October 2, 2005. The unique race was a 12-lap event with the top 10 Pro Open qualifiers and a mandatory pit stop. Joey Strub took the checkered flag.

• Each year drivers have an East/West Watercross Challenge. The win is based on combined points from two oval races—one making a counter-clockwise left turn (Western style) and one making a clockwise right turn (Eastern style). The 2005 win, for the fifth consecutive year, went to the East.

URLs

The International Watercross Association
   www.iwausa.org
WPSA Watercross
   www.wpsaracing.com
Grantsburg World Championship Watercross Races
   www.grantsburgwatercross.com
Henry Beida – Unofficial World Record Watercross Holder
   www.biedaspowersports.com/henry.html
SnowRider online magazine
   www.snowridermag.com

Sled #769, driven by Mike Smekens, is ahead of the Arctic Cat as they round the buoy. Notice the water pouring off his track creating a strong wake or wave, as well as water spray for the machine behind him.

Ever wondered what it's like to race a watercross oval class? This shot of #991, John Fleischman's Arctic Cat, gives a good idea of the reduced visibility from water spray, which acts just like snow dust on the ice oval course.

Going...going... It's easy to see when a snowmobile is having problems in watercross. The first thing that occurs is the sled starts to bounce on the water instead of holding a smooth line over the water.

Gone... This photo follows the last one as driver #123, Bruce Weaver, sinks in a heat race of his Semi Pro Open Oval class. While Memory Lake is fairly shallow, some watercross events are held in deep water, so the attached boat cushion the driver sits on floats to the surface to aid in locating the sunken snowmobile.

This is the retrieval boat that is specially designed to remove sunken snowmobiles from the water during a race event. The driver and rescue team attach the hoist to the sled and then pull it out of the water. In river racing or other deep water events divers are on standby to find the sled underwater. The retrieval boat takes the sled back to the pit area where mechanics get it started to try again in the next race.

Chad Maki, son of the watercross legend, Mark Maki, rides his #413 Ski-Doo in this class. In this 2005 photo Chas was just 14 years old racing his first season. He took two World Championship titles—Semi-Pro Stock Oval, and Stock 800 drags, along with the IWA 2005 Season Point Championships in the same classes.

These three Pro Open drivers are headed to the first buoy. Joey Strub rides the #3 Yamaha; Dale Lindbeck is in the center on his #29 Arctic Cat; and Ken Kolitsch is on the #175 Polaris. Lindbeck took his third World Championship of Watercross title in this 2005 event in Grantsburg, Wisconsin.

Jason McPheeters, #7, has his sled leaned into the corner around the buoy. Drivers on Western watercross circuits turn right (clockwise) to keep the clutch side of the sled up out of the water, while drivers on Eastern watercross circuits turn left (counter-clockwise) as they do in traditional ice oval racing events.

Jeff Fischer, on the Yamaha #2, looked to be the best hope in the East/West Challenge at Fremont, New Hampshire in 2005 until he ran into mechanical problems. The Challenge race runs half of the races clockwise and half counter-clockwise.

These two watercross drag racers are nearing the finish line. Travis Nelson is the Ski-Doo driver, #104.

Ken Kolitsch on the #175 Polaris stirs up the water as he's the first one around this part of the course. As the racers spread out on the watercross track it gets rougher and rougher as there is no time for the wake to disappear.

Jim Strub, Arctic Cat Driver #28, leads the way around the course. Notice how much water is in the air as three drivers all take different lines in this first lap of their heat race.

Andy Busse rides his #414 Ski-Doo in his Pro Stock Oval class. Spectators find watercross one of the most relaxing to attend, as they can often set up with all the comforts of home along the lakeshore or riverbanks.

More Great Titles From
Iconografix

All Iconografix books are available from direct mail specialty book dealers and bookstores worldwide, or can be ordered from the publisher. For book trade and distribution information or to add your name to our mailing list and receive a **FREE CATALOG** contact:

Iconografix, Inc.
PO Box 446, Dept BK
Hudson, WI, 54016

Telephone: (715) 381-9755,
(800) 289-3504 (USA),
Fax: (715) 381-9756
info@iconografixinc.com
www.iconografixinc.com

More great books from Iconografix

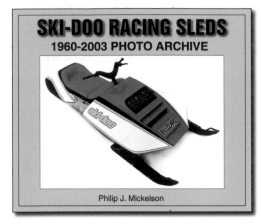
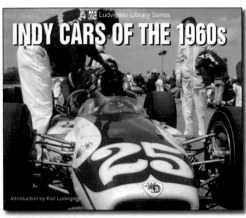
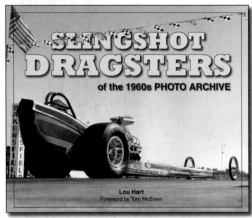

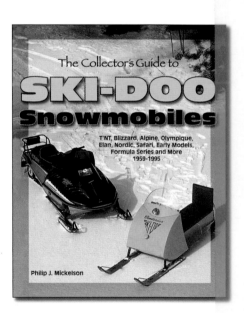
Iconografix, Inc.
P.O. Box 446, Dept BK,
Hudson, WI 54016
For a free catalog call: 1-800-289-3504
info@iconografixinc.com
www.iconografixinc.com